F-F-F-Frank Polk

Frank Polk

An Uncommonly Frank Autobiography

F-F-F-Frank Polk

Illustrated by Joe Beeler
with a Foreword by Slim Pickins

NORTHLAND PRESS / FLAGSTAFF

Dedicated to all the good cowboys I worked with,
all the good dudes I wrangled,
all the AA members who helped me,
and all the people I caused so much trouble to.

Contents

Foreword

IN 1975 I WAS A GUEST SPEAKER at the Cowboy Artists of America Show in Phoenix, Arizona. I talked then about a few of the many good times I'd had cowboyin' and makin' movies and about some of the funny things that have happened to me in the movie business. I remember pokin' fun at my friend Frank Polk when I told the audience there that "Frank's got a face that looks like it wore out three bodies." Frank's fellow Cowboy Artists really got a kick out of that.

Makin' a livin' cowboyin' and rodeoin' can be tough on a feller, and it takes someone with a strong constitution to stick to it. It takes this same kind of a feller, one who really knows how tough cowboyin' is, to portray a cowboy, whether it's on a movie set or in a wax model to be cast in bronze.

I first met Frank Polk in Reno in the late 1940s when I was rodeo clownin' and ridin' saddle broncs on the circuit. Frank was wranglin' dudes then and workin' on his wood carvings. It was tough in those days for a feller to make a livin' in the rodeo business. My friend Chuck Shepherd used to say that we starved to death together and had a good time doin' it.

Frank and I kept in touch over the years, seein' each other around the rodeo circuit now and again. In 1952 I remember rodeo clownin' at the Cow Palace in San Francisco and seein' Frank and our buddy Casey Tibbs. Frank had done a wood carving of Casey in honor of Casey's being the National Champion Bronc Rider that year.

I saw Frank years later in Jackson Hole, Wyoming, where I was making the movie *The Legend of Earl Durand*. We got to talkin' about sculpture and later we got together and Frank showed me some of the fine points of workin' with wax models. While workin' we spent hours together talkin' about people we'd known in the rodeo and motion picture business, and we told stories that kept us laughin' all the time.

Now I'm glad to see that Frank has written this book about his life of cowboyin', rodeoin', and workin' with his sculpture. Our friend Joe Beeler has done some great drawings to illustrate Frank's stories. I can sure see why they call this book Frank's "Uncommonly Frank Autobiography."

SLIM PICKINS

The Educated Burro
an' the Talkin' Kid

NOW I DON'T KNOW why they hung that name on me, 'cause I wasn't much of a talkin' kid. Didn't talk until I was five an' then I stammered after that. 'Course, guess I did talk a lot later on to make up for that poor start.

Well, you see, I was born near Louisville, Kentucky, in a little place they called Dogtown, where my grandmother had a boardin' house. You see, my folks lived in Indiana, but my mother went down to her mother's, like the old-fashioned way, to have her young 'un. So I was born there in Kentucky on September the first of nineteen hundred an' eight.

They tell me I'm kinda related to that President Polk. My mother said that was so, but I never had it looked up. You see, I didn't want it to happen like that feller who spent $5,000 to have his family tree looked up and $50,000 to have it shushed up.

$$K_4$$

About my earliest days there ain't a whole lot to say except that my father died when I was a young 'un an' my stepfather, Jim Bozell, was a travelin' barber. He would buy up a barbershop in one place, build it up an' sell it, an' then move on to do that in another town. He was always buyin' shops an' then sellin' them out an' movin' on to someplace else.

An' so finally we got to Phoenix right after World War I, and I graduated out of eighth grade from the old Monroe School. Before we knew it my stepdad sold out his shop there an' we came on up to Mayer. It was right here in Mayer that I started to high school. They only had the first an' second year. I liked school fine in Mayer, but soon we was a-movin' back to Phoenix where I had to go to that big high school.

Now I didn't like that school at all 'cause I was, I guess, kinda outa place. I never did understand why. I was dressin' the same way as I did when I went to school in Mayer—you know, big hat an' boots. An', like in Mayer, I rode my horse to school.

Never did understand why I had trouble with so many people down there in that big city.

When I was a kid I pretty much thought that if a guy wasn't a cowboy he just didn't amount to doodley-nothin'. So it wasn't long before I was out there learnin' to be a cowboy. I'd always been a pretty good hand with animals, teachin' dogs, horses, pigs an' other animals. Pretty soon I got a job with the little rodeos they put on around Phoenix in those days. I had a trained burro, an' they used to pay me five or ten dollars a day, which for a kid was quite a bit of money in those days. So I got to goin' to rodeos in a way, an' I got pretty much on the cowboys' side of it.

An' then I got to helpin' out there around Phoenix where they was shippin' in lots of cattle. I'd skip school an' go out there an' help 'em. An' heck, I'd get paid, too. So I got to ditchin' school, an' the principal sent a note to my mother tellin' her that I wasn't goin' to my classes. An' I said to my mother, "I'm goin' to quit school."

Like all old-time mothers, she meant well—she wanted me to have an education. But she said, "Well, if you're goin' to quit school, you've got to go to work."

[2]

I wasn't aimin' to cut my mother short, but I said, "Well, I already got me a job."

So there I was just a punk kid, about fourteen or fifteen, startin' out to be a cowboy. Like I said, a person who wasn't a cowboy to me didn't amount to doodley-nothin'.

ɤ

What I did want to tell you in the first place when I started out was how I got to that name, "The Educated Burro an' the Talkin' Kid."

You see, when we got up to Prescott where my brother Herman was a barber, too, I had a horse an' a burro an' dogs, an' I moved all my animals up with me. I got a job with the Prescott rodeo with my trained burro. I jist taught that burro all kinds of tricks—untie knots, lay down an' roll over; chase me an' bite at the seat of my pants, and all that stuff.

An' she could tell how old she was, an' just shut up, too. Which is what I ought to do now about my years as a kid.

All I can say is that burro surely was educated, an' I guess even with my stutterin' I was sure a talkin' kid in those days.

Jody Picked the Cotton

WELL, NOW, there I was, just a punk of a kid wantin' to be a cowboy, and I'd worked down there in the stockyards and the ranches around Phoenix. An' then I took my horses and went up to Prescott to get me a job cowboyin'.

That was the time when the Palace Bar on Whiskey Row was the main drag in Prescott an' all the ranchers an' all the cowboys hung out there. I'd heard that Clyde Miller, who ran the Yolo outfit up at Camp Wood, was hirin', an' that he was in the Palace Bar. So, heck, I walked in there an' I said to that man, "Mr. Miller, I hear you're lookin' for a man."

Now I was just a kid about fifteen or sixteen by that time. Well, he looked me up and down and he said, "Yeah, I'm lookin' for somebody." An', by golly, he hired me and took me up there to Camp Wood, where he put my horses out in pasture. That was my first job of workin' on what I call a big cowspread, where they had lots of bad horses an' lots of wild cattle.

When you're just a kid I guess you think you're purty smart an' you have to have lessons pounded into you the hard way. Like the time we were camped on the ol' Bozarth place on Bozarth Mesa.

I was puttin' an old shoe on a horse in my string. Now, you know when you're puttin' new nails in an ol' shoe they don't drive right down flush with the shoe, you see; the nail sticks out a little ways. Well, that ol' horse, that ol' son of a gun, stepped on me. He just come right down, stepped on my toe with that one nail. Well, that poked a hole in my boot an' that toe of mine just swelled up to a mountain.

There wasn't any of them cowboys around there, Orville or any of them, that was gonna help me. I jist had to go ahead an' finish shoein' that horse, an' afterwards I could hardly get my boot off. But Ol' Whistle, a cowboy up there, finally helped me an' even gave me an ol' pair of shoes to wear.

A kid can do some pretty dumb things. Like the time I remember we was comin' into the ranch with the holdup, about 200 cows, calves an' steers comin' in there. Ol' Clyde Miller had sent me in ahead. He said, "You go into the corral an' build a brandin' fire."

Well, I rode up ahead an' started shavin' some kindlin' for the fire. I was all set to build that fire, but I didn't have any matches. You see, I didn't smoke at that time. Well, I figured I'd jist wait 'til those cowboys came in.

So they came in and Miller says, "You ain't got no fire." He was mad. I could tell that, so I says quickly, "Well, I didn't have no matches."

Miller just shook his head. "It's only about a quarter of a mile up to the house. You could have gone up there to get some."

Well, I'd never thought of that. Like a dumb kid I'd just stood right there lookin' at that mess of wood shavin's. That's what a kid'll do.

3A

Now you might expect that man would've fired me right there an' then. But there wasn't much said about it, 'cause they knew I was a kid. I'll tell you, up there at Camp Wood was really a place a kid could learn about cowboyin'.

That job up there had only been temporary an' when we shipped the steers at Del Rio an' went into Prescott, ol' man Miller came up to me an' said, "Kid, how much do I owe you?"

I'd worked out there for two months. I didn't say anythin', I just stood there.

Miller said, "How much do I owe you?"

I looked up at him an' said, "Clyde (I was talkin' pretty big for a kid), as far as I'm concerned you don't owe me anythin'. I kinda liked it out there, an' now I got all that experience. An' if you look back at it, I wasn't too much of a hand."

Well, he says, "Frank, that's how we all learn. We all had to learn sometime."

Then he fished out his check book an' says, "Well, I'm payin' the other guys sixty dollars a month. How about payin' you forty-five dollars?"

"Suits me fine," I says.

He wrote me out a check for ninety dollars an' that was more money than I ever saw in my life. You know, I always admired that man.

◀C

I took that check and put that ninety dollars right in the bank, an' after that I floated around a bit, worked here an' there. An' I remember one incident about an ol' boy by the name of Purlie Morris who was clownin' the rodeo shows. He had a white mule—

called him Pinky. He was what you call an albino. Everythin' that showed was pink, but outside his hair was white. Even his goldurn sheath an' under his tail was all pink, you know. So that was his name, Pinky.

An' that Pinky bucked like a wild one an' Purlie asked me one day, "Frank, could you train that durn mule?"

You see, Purlie knew I was pretty good with trainin' animals, even though I was a kid. An' Purlie wanted that Pinky to be trained to work with him clownin' the rodeos.

O'l Purlie had made me a pair of blinds for that mule, but I forgot to take 'em when I rode Pinky back up to the ranch one day. So I used a red bandana for blinds. Tied one corner to one side of the bridle an' one corner of the rolled-up bandana to the

other side. An' heck, after I pulled the blinds he didn't buck with me but about one or two jumps until I was ridin' that mule down this road behind the cattle we was takin' back to Camp Wood. This kerchief that I'd used for blinds come loose on one side, swung around, an' hit that mule on the neck. Well, that mule jist bucked up through the cattle an' scattered the cattle all over the durned country. But he didn't buck me off, Pinky didn't. Later I trained him an', by golly, he became a pretty good mule that could do a lot of funny tricks.

Now, you see why they called me the Talkin' Kid. I been talkin' so much I plum forgot the story I started out to tell you.

Remember, I was tellin' you that they had a bunch of rough horses an' wild cattle up there at Camp Wood? An' Mr. Miller, why he cut me some of the goldurn roughest little horses you ever saw. An' one of those was a little ol' horse they called Jody Picked the Cotton. That was his name an' I'm not a-kiddin' you one bit, he was a dirty little son of a gun.

He wasn't so bad to buck so much, but gettin' on an' off he'd kick you, bite you, do anythin' else he could get away with. Well, I remember those older cowboys used to tell me to be a little more careful with that Jody 'cause he was about the worst horse around. Well, one time we was down there on South Mesa an' it was rainin'. I'd rolled up my slicker in a ball an' tied it on the back of my saddle. Actually it stuck up over the cantle.

We was workin' out there in the rain an' I had to go—pardon my expression—but I had to go, which in cowboy language meant I jist had to go take a crap, see? So I rode off to one side of the holdup an' started to step off this damned little ol' horse, an' I never thought about that slicker back of the saddle. An' damned if I didn't hang my leg on that goldurn slicker.

An 'that was the chance that Jody Picked the Cotton was a-waitin' for. He went out from under me an' kicked me in the belly with both hind feet. An' there I was layin' there on my back an' I couldn't breathe. Ol' Harry Knight and an ol' boy by the nickname of Whistle—Elton Mills was his proper name—come on over. An' I could hear ol' Whistle sayin' that he'd caught my horse " 'cause if Frank was dead we'd have to have some way to pack him back in."

Well, I jist couldn't catch my breath, an' finally I got Harry to hit me on the back so I could get my wind back. An' now I really had to go. I just had to pull my pants down an', by golly, I really took a big crap, to use that cowboy expression. Later on when ol' Whistle was tellin' that story an' makin' a big joke of it he'd say, "Frank, you made a pile two tall Indians couldn't shake hands over."

That story is still known like that today. They still tell it that ol' Jody Picked the Cotton kicked the shit out of Frank Polk down there on South Mesa.

A Gun Ain't Nothin'
to Fool Around With

IT DIDN'T TAKE ME LONG to learn that a gun ain't nothin' to fool around with.

I was about seventeen and was breaking horses for old Autty Lovelady. There was a kind'a argument over a brown horse we had. A guy the name of Fletcher came ridin' down to where me, Autty Lovelady, and his son Shorty was. This Fletcher came right up to the fence an' we saw he had a six-shooter stuck right down in his pants.

When ol' Autty saw him, he jumped right over that fence an' told Fletcher that the horse wasn't his. Ol' Autty says, "You haven't got a bill of sale and you jist ain't gonna take that horse."

Well, I was on the other side of the fence with Shorty an' I don't mind tellin' you, I was about half scared. I was lookin' right at that six-shooter. But there was Autty right alongside that Fletcher, right up close to that six-shooter, an' Autty says again, "You ain't takin' this horse."

An', by golly, if that ol' boy Fletcher didn't get back on his horse and jist ride off.

When Autty had climbed back over that fence I asked him why he'd taken the chance of gettin' right up close to that man with the gun.

"Well," Autty says, "I was born an' raised in Texas an' learned about this kind of deal right quick. If a guy's ever got a gun an' you don't have one, jist get as close to him as you can. If he ever makes a pass for that gun, why you hang one on him. Yes, sir, just hang one on him."

To tell the truth, I never was one for guns, but I can remember one incident up at Rainbow Lodge when I came up against a situation where I almost used one.

I was riding a mule called Kate, an' she was a pretty good mule. I'd taken a lot of pains makin' a good mule out of her. An' there was this ol' boy from down around Cornville who was, I guess, a little on the crazy side. Well, he wanted to ride her. You see, if you're ridin' a certain animal yourself you don't want anybody else foolin' with her. So I says, "I don't want you ridin' that mule. There's lots of mules there in the corral."

But no, he was goin' to ride that mule Kate.

I says, "By God, you're not goin' to ride her." I was only about twenty-one then, an' pretty hotheaded.

An' he says, "Goldurn it, I am."

I says, "To hell you are." An' then I jist jumped over the corral fence an' hung one on him.

He started on up the hill, cursin' an' throwin' rocks at me on the way up. An' when he got to the house he says, "I'm goin' to get my six-shooter an' I'm goin' to come down an' shoot the hell out of you."

I says, "You jist go ahead."

Well, he went on up to the bunkhouse an' I turned an' headed for the tradin' post. An' I got me a thirty-thirty. I never was much for guns, but I did get that gun an' put some shells in it. I walked out of that tradin' post an' headed back down where I could watch this door of the bunkhouse. I honestly believe if he'd walked out of there with that gun I'd have shot him. I got to thinkin' about what I might have done an' it kind'a scared me. If he'd of walked out of there an' I'd have shot him I'd have been sorry about it all the rest of my life.

☌

Now, I never owned a gun. I've never had too much to do with guns. I've taken a couple of guns away from guys to keep 'em from shootin' people. There was the time that I'd had a fight with Bill, a big ol' tall guy. Afterwards he got to packin' a durned gun around in his jeans.

I told him, "Bill, you do one of two things. You either pull that gun out an' start shootin' or else quit packin' it around."

For a little while I wasn't sure whether he was gonna pull it on me or not. But, by golly, he did quit packin' that gun around from that day on.

A guy that packs a gun an' don't want to use it ain't got no business packin' it at all. Because you know what will happen to him? Somebody will shoot *him,* that's what!

The Days an' Nights
of a Cowboy

THERE AIN'T A WEEK GOES BY when somebody doesn't ask me what it was like cowboyin' in my days. They expect to hear a lot of wild an' woolly stories because they've been lookin' at cowboys on television and on the movie screens. If you wanted to be a cowboy today you'd have a helluva time with all those fences they've strung around.

Before all this country was fenced up this was all open range an' there'd be one big outfit that was kinda ramroddin', and other smaller ones where the cattle would all run together. An' when they had this spring works, or the fall works, why everybody worked together brandin' the calves an' gettin' the steers they wanted to sell. In those days they didn't sell calves. A steer wasn't sold until he was at least two years old.

We worked pretty hard in those days. You got up pretty early in the mornin'. When you was makin' the long drives you was pretty near to the head of your drive when the sun came up. You rolled out of the sack about four o'clock or half-past four. Heck, I've seen the time down there in Bloody Basin where everybody was strikin' matches out in the corral while tryin' to catch their horses. There's a little story about that I'd like to tell you.

There was one cowboy that came out to work on the Horseshoe Ranch when we was camped in Bloody Basin at the LX Bar. The outfit was camped down below a ridge. One day this new

{ 13 }

cowboy rode up on the ridge and said to the others, "Hey, what's that place down there?"

The cowboys chuckled an' one of them says, "Well, that's your camp. You've been camped there for five days."

That other feller scratches his head an' says, "Well, I wouldn't recognize it. I never saw it in the daylight."

OK

I get all charged up when I see these cowboy movies on the television. They're always sittin' around a campfire eatin'. Well, that's a lot of hooey. You didn't do a lot of eatin'; you did a lot of ridin'. We ate before we left camp in the mornin'—steak an' potatoes, biscuits an' gravy—an' we ate of an evenin'. Some guys would

put three or four sticks of jerky in their chap pocket, but the trouble was a lot of these outfits you worked for was short of water an' a lot of guys wouldn't eat that jerky because it makes you mighty thirsty. The fact is you never ate durin' the day; you were busy an' a person never bothered eatin'.

When you came back in you had all you wanted to eat—steak, potatoes, and beans. Those ol' camp cooks would usually have this log cabin syrup an' biscuits, which the cowboys called "lick." If you wanted somethin' sweet you just took some canned milk, mixed in sugar an' poured it on biscuits. Those ol' camp cooks used to make what they called tallow puddin'. They'd make it when they'd butcher a beef an' they'd take the tallow off and boil it. Haven't seen a tallow puddin' in years.

ᴜᴘ

When I first started cowboyin' I didn't get but forty-five dollars a month. Then they raised the wages up to where you was gettin' sixty dollars. An' along towards the late 1920s when they was really workin' lots of cattle they raised the wages to seventy-five dollars. An' if you wanted to ride the rough string—some outfits always had a lot of bad horses—you got paid ninety dollars a month.

Then durin' the Depression in the thirties, it got back down to where they was payin' only forty-five a month. If a guy was gettin' sixty dollars, he was gettin' a lot of money.

In those days you got paid when you came to town to ship the cattle. An', I guess some people saved, but not many cowboys I knew ever did. What they did was spend it all on a good time. Like a guy I remember by the name of Bruce Barnes. One day a guy was askin' him what he did with his money. So Bruce says he was investin' all his money in real estate.

An' this other feller says, "Well, that's pretty good. What kind of real estate?"

"Oh," says Bruce, "I invest in houses an' lots."

The other feller asks, "Well, where is that?" Guess he thought he could get in on a good deal.

An' Bruce answers him, "Well, I invest in *houses* of ill fame an' *lots* of whiskey."

That's the kind of investments a lot of us cowboys would make when we came into Prescott, which in those days was the Cowboy Capital of the World. It was a pretty rough town. I guess I've seen more fights down there on Whiskey Row in the four days they had the rodeo than you could see in four days in any town in the U.S.A.

Prescott was a kind'a wide-open town. They had a lot of fights an' I guess somebody usually got killed during the Fourth of July. But they didn't bother you; they didn't shut the town down on you. An' actually there was a reason for it.

You see, cowboys did a lot of drinkin' an' gamblin' an' fight-in', but there never was any girls molested. As far as anythin' crim-inal happenin'—rapes or anythin' like that—well, it jist didn't happen. When a cowboy came to town the first thing he did was to go to the Palace Barbershop where they had four bathtubs. He'd take a bath and change clothes. He probably hadn't had a bath all during the spring works, maybe for two months. An' then he'd jist go out an' have a purty good time of it, an' he didn't seem to care what happened.

There was this friend of mine they called Moonlight Jimmy 'cause he once rode a buckin' horse on a bet on a moonlight night. Well, I remember one night we went into Prescott an' we were settin' down there on the curb of this ol' Mason Hotel, which really was a whorehouse run by a gal the name of Gabe. Moonlight Jimmy was settin' there on the curb playin' his ukulele, or some-thin', an' we was singin' an' passin' the bottle around.

All of a sudden this sheriff came over an' started raisin' a tune to run us all off. Ol' Moonlight Jim was purty drunk, an' he gave that sheriff an argument an' in the middle of it, he hung one on that sheriff. He jist floored that man.

Well, they throwed Moonlight Jimmy in the county jail for six months. He was a comical son of a gun an' when he finally got out of jail all his friends was kiddin' him. Moonlight Jimmy jist says, "Hell, it ain't no disgrace to be in that place. It's the biggest house in town."

Those Were Good Ol' Gals

NOW I WANT TO TELL YOU that a cowboy had an awful lot of respect for women. He had a respect for ranchers' daughters an' women in town. Cowboys never really got to courtin' town gals very much 'cause they wasn't around long enough to make acquaintances.

I seen guys in cow camps sittin' around talkin'. You could talk about whores, talk about anythin' in the world. Call a guy a dirty son of a bitch or dirty bastard, or any goldurn thing in the world. But if you talked about somebody's wife, or somebody's girl, you had a fight on your hands right there. That kind'a talk was taboo, strictly taboo.

Of course, there wasn't nothin' wrong with talkin' about the whores and whorehouses in town. A lot of times cowboys would say that the height of their ambition was movin' into a town an' ownin' a whorehouse. Remember hearin' a couple of cowboys talkin' about it. "Well, goldurn it, let's move into town an' we'll start us a whorehouse. Why, until we get us some girls, we'll just run the darn place by hand."

There was one ol' married cowboy who was in the barbershop a-gettin' his hair cut, an' another ol' boy in the other chair was a-gettin' his cut, too. In those days they used to put a lot of tonic on your hair.

One of the barbers asked this first guy if he'd like to have him put some tonic on his hair an' he says, "No, hell no, I get that on an' I go home an my wife will think I smell just like a whorehouse, damn it."

An' so the other barber asks the other ol' boy sittin' in his chair if he wants any tonic on his hair. An' he says, "Hell yes, put it on. My wife don't know what a whorehouse smells like."

ED

It was a funny thing, but every gal that run a whorehouse would pick out one cowboy that was kind'a her man an' that cowboy would begin to think she was the greatest thing in the world. Now, I can't say that was stupid 'cause a lot of those ol' gals were really nice. I mean, if you was broke or somethin', they'd always feed you, or give you a drink, or anythin' else you might need.

Of course, there's a lot of guys that was kind'a taken in by some of those gals. I can name a few of those cowboys, but I don't think I will. Some of 'em might have married those gals. Heck, I know several guys that married their whores, an' to be truthful, they turned out to be darn good wives. There was one gal there in Prescott that run a whorehouse. That gal had some children and she had to make a livin' for those kids so she just got to runnin' this here whorehouse. An' I'll tell you she was a pretty nice ol' gal. In fact, she had a man who I worked for later; he was her cowboy. Later on she married an ol' boy from Prescott, closed her whorehouse, and they say she made that ol' boy as good a wife as you ever saw.

Now there's a lot of difference between a good gal an' those damned drunken chippies. You got to understand that. An' they didn't all get married either. I know one gal ran a house down in Phoenix. This friend of mine had that as his favorite house an' he always went down there to be with that same whore. They never had the idea of gettin' married an' raisin' a family. They just enjoyed doin' what they were doin'.

There was quite a famous ol' gal up there in Prescott. Gabe was her name, an' she was quite well known. They even wrote a story about her. Called it "The Girl in the Red Kimona," or "The Scarlet Robe," an' they made a picture of it.

Well, I remember this particular time when we were all up there at Gabe's havin' a helluva time drinkin' bootleg whiskey they sold up there at the whorehouse. These guys were drinkin' an' doin' a lot of talkin' about the bad horses they'd rode while cowboyin'. An' they just kept on talkin' about what they'd done out there workin' on ranches, an' stayin' in camps. An' that was kind'a

funny, 'cause out in the cow camp they was always a-talkin' about the whorehouses, yappin' about how good this whore was and how bad this other one was—which one was the best lay an' which one wasn't. Now don't get me wrong, they wasn't runnin' the whores down. That's just what the conversation was about out there at the cow camp. But now here they were in the whorehouse an' what were they talkin' about? Talkin' a mile a minute about tyin' up this big steer, runnin' this ornery one down an' so on. An' all the time they was talkin' about cowboyin' Gabe's gals were jist sittin' around.

Gabe came in and saw that situation. Those gals were not doin' what they was intended for. So she says to those cowboys, "Now you guys just make up your mind. You come up here to this whorehouse an' you set around an' you're ridin' every bad horse out on the ranch; you're workin' all the bad an' wild cattle. Now you look here, this whorehouse ain't no ranch. This whorehouse is a place to do your screwin'. Listen to me, when you're out at the ranch do your cowboyin' an' do your screwin' when you're up here in the whorehouse. These gals ain't gonna make no money sittin' around; they got to turn tricks. Now get your things straightened around. Each one of you get you a gal an' get goin'."

HK

I knew a pretty good ol' gal who was a whore. As I said, she was a nice ol' gal, but there was a funny thing about her. Tattooed on her belly was the words "Pay as You Enter." I thought that was pretty funny an' one time I jist up an' asked why she had that tattooed there. An' she told me. She said there were times she got drunk, an' she thought that would make a pretty good reminder for her customers!

They Called Me "Peaceful Polk"

NOW I WANT TO TELL YOU about one of the funniest outfits I ever worked for. I was up there at Camp Wood helpin' my best friend, Dave Hill. This was durin' the Depression, an' I was wantin' to get a payin' job. So I heard there was a couple of fellers by the name of Les Jenkins and Casey Jones who was gathering a remnant of wild cattle. I heard they was kind'a short of help, so I told Dave, "I think I'll go down there an' see if they want to hire somebody."

Well, I saddled up a horse an' I rode down there about thirty miles down to their camp. I rode into that camp, an' that was the goldurnest thing I ever did see. All them guys had—an' I'm tellin' the truth—was a five-gallon keg of whiskey, a sack of jerky an' a sack 'a flour. That's all the commodities they had. It was a wild outfit, an' I guess they just stayed drunk all the time. So I went up to this ol' Les Jenkins, an' he says to me, "We can't afford to hire nobody. We're just tryin' to get these durn wild cattle out of here."

So I said, "Well, hell, I'll just stay down here an' help."

Well, we trapped a lot of cattle an' led 'em out of there. An' ol' Jenkins, he got so drunk one day he fell off his horse an' we had to go find him 'cause his horse came in without him.

I'll tell you that was jist a funny doggoned outfit. I stayed with that outfit until the whiskey ran out, an' later I'd tell the story on 'em—that all they had in the world was a five-gallon keg of whiskey, a sack of jerky an' a sack of flour!

{ 24 }

3

There was the time, to be truthful, when I was livin' down near the bootleggin' joints in Prescott. Just livin' there an' stayin' drunk. Well, the Perkins outfit from Texas was lookin' for someone to ride a string of rough horses that other cowboys couldn't ride. An' this feller Chappo told Nick Perkins, his boss, "I know an ol' boy who can ride those horses." An' he came an' got me.

I didn't have a saddle, not a durn thing from all that drinkin'. But Chappo let me have his saddle, an' the first night I was out there on the ranch I wasn't in the best shape after all that drinkin'.

But it didn't take me long after they'd cut me twelve head of horses an' that next afternoon I went out there an' started shoein' that bunch of horses. In those days a cowboy that couldn't shoe a horse didn't work. I laid every horse on his side, tied down, to shoe him.

Now I had these rough horses to ride, an' I went to a bronc ride every day for about two weeks. I really knocked it out of those goldurn horses, 'cause that was really up my alley. One day, ol' Nick Perkins—I tell you he was the best durn cowman I ever knew—came up to me an' said, "We're movin' to the horse camp and I got a horse I want you to ride if we can find him."

I said, "All right, fine." An' I never thought anythin' about it, at least not until I saw that horse. He was a big ol' sorrel horse, an' he had the biggest goldurned head that I ever saw. I knew right away that ol' Nick was jobbin' me, and I figured that ol' horse had bucked a lot of cowboys off. Well, I kind'a put off ridin' that horse 'til we moved back to the ranch but ol' Nick stayed after me. One afternoon when we were down on the flat country along the Verde River, Nick said to me, "This is a pretty good time for you to ride that ol' Jerry."

That was it. I went out there an' saddled that big ol' horse in the corral, an' I stepped up on him. I said to that goldurn horse, "If you've got any buck in you, get it out right now."

Well, you know, it was funny, I couldn't get a buck out of that horse; he was just nice an' quiet.

A couple of days later I was ridin' that horse alongside ol' Nick an' we was talkin' about things when all of a sudden that horse really fell apart. God almighty, he sure bucked like a son of a gun. I really went to work on him. I spurred the hell out of that durned horse. An' I could hear ol' Nick ridin' behind me an' hollerin', "Don't spur him in the shoulders! Don't spur him in the shoulders!"

Well, I remember I looked back an' said, "Well, to hell with you, you ol' son of a gun. You been tryin' to job me on this durned horse all the time."

An' as I was sayin' that the goldurn horse quit buckin'. I rode that horse many times after that an I tried to make him buck, but he would never buck any more with me; I could do anythin' with that horse. All that horse needed was someone to knock it out of him.

They tell me that up to the time he died Nick Perkins was still talkin' about how Frank Polk rode that ol' Jerry.

There was some pretty hard times out there cowboyin' and sometimes it was even harder in town. I remember one time we went up to that Mason Hotel, that ol' whorehouse in Prescott, an' we was drinkin' up a storm there. I'd already had a couple of fights, an' here were these bellhops that had come over from the Hassayampa Hotel. One little guy was really wantin' to fight. Well, we got to fightin' an' I cooled him out over in a corner with a quick left, an' I was gettin' ready to really work him over when this friend of mine, a great big feller named Chick Reynolds, came over.

He said, "Now you got him whipped. That's enough." An' he jist picked this feller up by the collar an' the seat of his pants. Well, about this time the gals had come out in the hall an' they was a-wringin' their hands, a-worryin' about the cops comin' up there. So Chick asked the gals, "Well, what do you want me to do with him?"

One of the gals was real excited an' she pointed to the stairs. She meant to jist get him out of the hotel, but Chick jist threw that little feller right down the stairs. I'll tell you, I sobered up mighty quick when that guy landed at the bottom. I thought, "That guy's sure enough killed." Well, we went down an' picked him up an' carried him clear back upstairs to a room an' put him to bed. We made up between us that if he was dead we'd agree to say that he fell down the stairs. Well, durned, if about two hours later that guy don't come walkin' in to where we was. An' you know what? He didn't have a skinned place on him! That fall would've been enough to kill the guy—if he'd been sober.

+U

That drinkin' got me into a lot of fights, an' there was one time I got in a fight with my wife Mary's brother, Roy Cooper. He kind'a liked to fight, too. Well, we was out there at this dance an' everyone, it seemed, had a gallon jug of bootleg whiskey.

I found out after Roy had broken my jaw in the fight that he thought I had spit in his wife Nell's face. But actually what had happened was that I had stuttered an' kind'a sprayed her unintentionally.

Well, the mornin' after that fight with Roy, me an' my buddy Dave Hill wound up at the Palace lookin' for a drink. We was both of us sick an' we needed a drink. Well, we knew there was some guys in a room who had some whiskey, so we went there an' I knocked on the door. A guy by the name of Fay Harbison comes to the door an' asks, "Who's out there?"

Now, I don't know what made me say it, but I says, "Last night it was ol' Fightin' Frank, but this mornin' it's jist ol' Peaceful Polk."

Well, they let us in, gave us drinks an' you know for years after they called me Peaceful Polk.

Ridin' Broncs
an' Drinkin' Don't Mix

A LOT OF COWBOYS DRANK. I mean a lot of 'em could handle their whiskey, but I think them prohib days was bad, 'cause you got hold of a bottle an' you had to get rid of it fast so you wasn't caught. Golly, you an' three or four other guys would kill a bottle of that bootleg in about three or four drinks. That's where really an' truly I think a lot of alcoholics developed. If you could've gone into a bar an' set there an' talked an' taken a drink, why that would have been better. But in those day you sure killed a bottle quick.

It wasn't hard findin' that bootleg whiskey. I remember up there at Sheep Creek there was a bunch of Mexicans an' they had a still up there. They made this whiskey an' they'd bring it down to Phoenix to sell. But they were pretty smart fellers. They'd load up their wagons with wood an' then they'd hide four or five kegs of whiskey under that load.

Up there at Camp Creek there was an' ol' guy who was kind'a bootleggin' to all the cattle outfits around. When we'd hit the river, the Verde, somebody'd always go ahead an' bring back a jug of that ol' man's whiskey. We didn't stay dry too long a spell.

Sometimes you had to be careful who you was drinkin' with 'cause there was these stool pigeons who would drink with you an' then turn you in. Like the time I was up at Mormon Lake at the rodeo with my buddy, ol' Dave Hill. We was together so much they called us the Gold Dust Twins. I guess they called us that 'cause we was always together an' gettin' in trouble. When you saw one of us, you saw the other. Heck, in those days cowboys kind'a paired up in a certain way. You always kind'a had a partner, some ol' boy that you worked with, rode with, an' traveled with—an' I guess got drunk with.

What it was about Dave is that he could sure start fights, but he couldn't fight at all, an' I guess that's one of the reasons I got in

a lot of fights. I remember one summer we was movin' all over the state, drinkin' pretty good an' enterin' all the rodeos, big an' small. We was up at Mormon Lake for this rodeo an' I guess I was drinkin' pretty heavily. I couldn't eat much, but I sure could drink that ol' whiskey; it didn't seem to bother me. It was right after the horse fell on me in Prescott, an' I wasn't in very good shape, but I won the bronc ridin' over there anyway. Right afterwards my buddy an' I would go out in the pine trees to get some of that bootleg whiskey. I guess it was ol' Bob Burch who had that whiskey out there in the trees. An' so we was goin' out there to fill a bottle with that goldurn stuff. The night before one of those prohibs—one of those stool pigeons—had got drunk with us, an' then, dammit, if he didn't turn in the guy who had sold us the whiskey.

Well, we got that bottle of whiskey an' we was comin' out of the pines when here come these officers. An' golly, I had this bottle of whiskey stuck down in my goldurn pants; that's where you always carried a bottle. Well, those agents got me out of one side of the car an' I quickly sneaked around the other side and hid that bottle behind a goldurn pine tree. Well, those prohibs searched us an' couldn't find a thing. Believe me, they was really upset. They took off in one direction an' we took off in the other—with that bottle.

LX

You do a lot of damn foolish things when you're drinkin'. Like the time I went down into Prescott jist drinkin' an' raisin' hell. I was ridin' my horse on the sidewalks an' I even rode him into Shell Dunbar's Palace Bar. It seems like the police didn't care for that one bit an' they throwed me in jail, an' damn if it didn't cost me. I got a ninety-day suspended sentence. Turned out one of the ranchmen needed me to work an' he came to town an' got me.

But a little while later I came on back to town where I'd been courtin' this lady—Threedy—who lived down at the Head Hotel.

At the Prescott Rodeo in 1932, Frank had the best
ride of the day on a saddle bronc named Streak

Well, my buddy, ol' Dave Hill, was the night clerk there. One
night he got himself so durn drunk he was a ravin' maniac. I took
him out to this little ranch out of town that Threedy owned, an' I
really worked to sober him up. He was surely a mess. Finally I got
him sobered, but durn if I didn't go on a big drunk, an' it wasn't
long before Dave was tryin' to help sober me up.

I got so bad Dave called that Sheriff Bozarth an' Dave says,
"You better come an' get ol' Frank. He's up at the Head Hotel
drunk as hell an' about to have a fit. I can't call the police 'cause
he's got a ninety-day suspended sentence hangin' over his head in
the city."

Well, Dave jist suggested they put me in the county jail,

which they did, an' he came down to see me. He said to me, "Now, they're jist goin' to sober you up. That's all they're goin' to do, an' then I'll come on down an' get you out."

So they was tryin' to sober me up slowly an' the deputy was slippin' around the back an' bringin' me a big ol' glass of wine about every two hours.

Well, when I went before the county judge I was pretty sober, an' my buddy Dave was there with me. An' I'll be darned if that judge didn't give me a ninety-day suspended sentence. So there I was, ninety days out of the county jail an' ninety days suspended sentence out of the city jail. It didn't take lightnin' to strike me to figure they jist wanted to get me the hell out of town; they'd had enough of ol' Frank Polk.

So durn if ol' Sid DeSpain, one of the sheriff's deputies, didn't take me down to the bus headin' out of town. An' the last thing he let me do before I got on that bus was to buy a pint of whiskey.

You know, back around 1936 I had to quit rodeoin' on account of my drinkin'. I was a pretty good rider an' I won a little money sometimes. But I found out that rodeoin' an' drinkin' jist don't mix too good. So I jist quit ridin' broncs.

So when I started back rodeoin' in 1941, I made up my mind never to take a drink until after the show was over. But if I did win, I sure tied one on afterwards.

Rocky's Nose Was Durn Near as Big as Mine

MULES IS SMARTER than horses, an' burros is smarter than horses, too. Burros are born with what you call a sense of self-preservation. They're born to really look after themselves. They're not real stubborn, as people think. A burro ain't gonna run himself to death. But a horse will run himself absolutely to death.

Now, they crossed a burro an' a horse an' that's what they call a mule; they got part of the horse an' part of the burro. An' that's why people had a lot of trouble gettin' along with mules 'cause they tried to treat a mule just like they treat a horse. Up there at the Grand Canyon, where I was a guide, we used to feed those mules in troughs. We'd just empty a whole sack of grain down this trough. One of 'em could eat as much as he wanted to. Now a horse in that same place would founder himself; he'd eat himself to death. A mule would eat so much an' quit. Now, whether you can call that smart, or born with an instinct for self-preservation, I can't say. But those are the facts about mules.

§

I learned a lot about mules in my days, an' that brings up a kind'a funny incident. I was up there in northern Arizona takin' pack trips to Rainbow Bridge, and one time we had the Rockefeller family on a pack trip. There was John D. II an' all his sons, an' one of their cousins, and they had their doctor with them, too.

Nelson Rockefeller—I guess they call him Rocky now—was about my age then. About twenty, I guess. An' David was the little fat one. I'll never forget him. On the trip over to Rainbow Bridge that David had a big deal. He had one of those butterfly nets with him, an' heck, before you knew it he'd get off his mule an' go chasin' off after butterflies. An' I'd have to jump off an' go after him and bring him back.

An' that Nelson, why he's got a pretty-good-sized nose, you know, just like I have. And that goldurn big nose of his jist got as sunburnt as could be 'cause he never wore a hat. Well, you never saw what that doc they had with them fixed up for Rocky. He'd

taken a piece of balin' wire, an' some gauze an' some adhesive tape, an' goldurn if he didn't make a nose shade for Nelson. It come right down over his nose—it looked like a big old beak sticking out there. An' he wore that thing all the way. For three days he wore that goldurn thing on his nose. That was the funniest thing I ever saw.

O

One time I packed the whole Fox picture outfit down there. They was makin' that picture called *The Rainbow Trail* with George O'Brien and Sue Carroll; they was starrin' in it. Well, I packed 'em in an' packed 'em out an' I had to cook for all of them, too. Goin' down there's a place called Redbud Pass, jist wide enough for jist an ordinary pack to go through. We had this one mule packed with those big cameras an' we had to be awful careful so that mule didn't bump goin' through the pass. Well, I was scared, so I unpacked that mule an' carried the cameras through that narrow pass. Then I got that dirty son of a gun packed again an' started along the trail again.

But I'll be durned if that mule didn't spook an' fall over into the canyon, landin' right on top of those cameras. It wasn't too far down, about ten feet; but when I looked, all I could see was those four feet stickin' up in the air. An' golly, I thought them cameras was really wrecked. When I got down there I saw those cameras wasn't hurt a bit; the pack had been so tight, it didn't even turn.

S̲

The movie company decided to stay a couple of extra days for shootin' down by the bridge an' we goldurn near run out of chuck. Actually all we had left was canned tomatoes an' fruit an' fixin's for biscuits. Well, I guess I jist cooked up a storm of biscuits an' that's why them movie people nicknamed me "Biscuits."

【 36 】

There was one time I remember, about 1926, when I was comin' off a pretty good drunk. I was workin' for a mule tradin' outfit in Phoenix an' handlin' lots of mules an' deliverin' them to the cotton farmers. This feller who worked for the park service up at the Grand Canyon had come down to buy mules for those pack trains up at the canyon, an' he told me that if I ever wanted a job up there to come on up. Well, if I do say so, I was an awful good hand with mules. I mean, you know, I'd been handlin' 'em ever since I was a kid with that—remember—with that educated burro an' that mule Pinky. So I wound up at the Grand Canyon.

Well, that kind'a brings me around to a funny incident that happened when we was packin' down to the bottom of the Grand Canyon. In those days they had that ol' suspension bridge. It was made out of wood an' had slats on the side, an' actually you could put only one mule at a time across that bridge. We had an ol' mule called Cotton an' he was one of the dirtiest ol' mules I ever saw. We didn't pack him unless we really had to.

This one time we had to take all this lumber down an' we

needed that ol' mule. The wood was in planks, cut about eight foot in length, an' you put 'em on the lumber bunk an' they had what you called a lumber hitch. Anyway, the lumber bunk stuck out on the side. I was in front of the pack string an' I would hold 'em up 'til the man in back would tie his mule up an' come to the front. Then I would go on across, and then he would send the pack mules across one at a time. Well, this time I'd done what I was supposed to, an' I had tied up the mule ahead of Cotton when he sent this ol' Cotton across.

This Cotton came a-flyin'. That son of a gun was pretty near on top of me. I had my back turned when I heard him comin'. It was about sixty feet down to the river, but I didn't think twice when I saw that ol' mule. I jist jumped off the side an' grabbed for that cable. I hung on for dear life while that durn ol' Cotton ran by. I got back on the trail an' caught him an' tied him up. When I got that Cotton back up on top in the corral I sure worked him over.

He was a dirty ol' son of a gun, that Cotton.

ORO

An' there was another time when we was haulin' dynamite down to the river bottom. Of course, you made sure you never packed your caps an' dynamite in the same mule train. You packed three boxes of dynamite on a mule, two on the sides an' one on top. We was takin' a box of caps down an' packed ol' Hattie with those caps on top of a pack 'cause she was a good ol' mule. We come down the trail all right, an' after we come off that bridge, there was this big, sandy beach. I don't know what got into that ol' Hattie, but when she got down in that sand she jist started to buck. I don't know what in the world ever happened to her, but there she was, a-buckin' away with that box of caps on top of her. She was right behind me, an' I was tryin' to get out of the way quick as I could.

Well, I took off runnin' in that sand an 'that ol' mule was just a-followin' me, buckin' an' hangin' behind me with that box full of caps. Those caps was dangerous an' I guess I made two full circles with ol' Hattie behind me before we got her stopped. Whew! Now that was quite a little incident.

MT

Now that story kind'a reminds me of another time when we was packin' a bunch of students in a hikin' club from that college at Flagstaff down to Rainbow Bridge. They had all their backpacks, but I had to pack all their food an' the other stuff they couldn't carry. I had decided to ask the daughter of the cook at the lodge to ride down with me on this pack trip. This gal was about twenty-eight, an' I guess I was twenty-one, but I got to courtin' her pretty good anyway.

I packed up the mules, an' this one mule I had was packed with a box of oranges on one side, a box of apples on the other, an' a case of eggs on the top. I packed two other mules, too, an' we took off down the trail. Now, I couldn't talk to this girl with those mules in between us, so I just turned 'em loose. I guess I wasn't payin 'too much attention to those mules. I was talkin' to that little gal, you know, courtin' her, an' we came off this ridge toward this other canyon.

I could look down below, an' see this ol' mule, Coyote. He got to trottin' an' the sack of tin dishes on top of him got to rattlin', an' darned if he didn't get to buckin'. The cans with bread in 'em came off, and Coyote would kick 'em in the air, jist like footballs. I was sittin' up high an' those mules was down below me, an' suddenly I seen ol' Coyote run into this other mule with the eggs, the oranges, an' the apples on her. That mule went to buckin', an' here was them two mules a-buckin', an' pretty soon those apples an' them oranges an' eggs got to flyin' in the air.

That was the funniest thing you ever did see—apples a-flyin' in one direction, the oranges in the other. Why, I figured those eggs was finished for good. But when we got down there it was the goldurnedest thing you ever saw. Those eggs had landed in their layers in the bushes, an' we ended up with about half of them eggs unbroken!

Now takin' those dudes down to Rainbow Bridge on those mules in 1929 was somethin' a man jist doesn't forget. Golly, I had an ol' mule up there by the name of Dinah, an' she was a dirty ol' son of a gun to shoe. An' one time I was takin' these boys to the bridge an' I jist happened to look back an' here was this one boy off this mule called Dinah. He had her hind foot picked up, an' I says to myself, "Oh, my God! That ol' mule's gonna kick that boy down into the canyon."

I run back there, an' that boy says to me, "She was limpin'. I think she's got a rock fastened in her foot."

I said, "There's nothin' the matter with that mule. Drop that foot an' get back on her."

I didn't say nothin' more, but I tell you, if it had been me that picked up her foot on that trail, Dinah would have kicked me plumb off that trail an' down into the canyon. I guess the good Lord looks after all drunken fools and children.

There's a lot of damn fools in this world, an' I met a bunch of 'em up there at the Grand Canyon when I was guidin' in 1935. Every summer there was these hikers who thought they could climb down an' get back out of the canyon. An' sure enough they'd make it down but when they started back up it would be hot, an' they'd pull a hamstring or somethin' else an' couldn't get out. So we'd have to go down the trail an' bring 'em out. That's what they called a dragout.

One time it was my turn for the dragout an' I had got me a pint of whiskey an' started down the trail ridin' one mule an' leadin' another. I really had that lead mule's neck stretched out 'cause I was goin' down that trail in a hurry, an' I got down to Indian Gardens an 'here this ol' boy was settin' down, an' he couldn't straighten his legs out. They were just all cramped in under him. I couldn't figure out how to get him on that mule an' get him on up the trail. Finally I got him up on top of a big rock an' I got the mule in under him. I just kind'a pushed him off the rock an' onto that mule.

Now, that was quite a sight bringin' that dude up the trail an' out of the canyon.

ᚱ

That kind'a led to another incident. It was pretty late when I got that dude up to the top, an' at that time I was doin' some entertainin' in a show we had up there in front of the Bright Angel Lodge every evening.

Well, I was tired from haulin' that guy out of the canyon so I went up to the Bright Angel an' ate an' had a few drinks. I guess I was pretty well kicked up. Well, about that time here came the superintendent of that ol' Fred Harvey up there an' he says, "Say, don't you know they've got that show goin' on out there?"

An' I says, "I just had a dragout an' I'm tired an' I'm gonna eat my dinner. I'll be out there at the show after I finish." Well, you know how the big boss is. I finally got out there an' sang an' played the guitar along with Barney Iles who was a natural-born comedian. He could really play one of those broomstick fiddles. He was a comical son of a gun, but he wasn't too much of a guide.

I remember one time when he went down to Phantom Ranch on a mule trip with this lady. They stayed down there overnight

an' the next day Barney came out ridin' the mule the lady was supposed to be ridin', an' the lady was ridin' Barney's mule. He was a
comical guy, but he didn't know one mule from another.

Anyhow, what I wanted to tell you is that the boss was jist
ready to dress me down after that show. But I got the first word in.
I says, "You're not payin' anybody enough up here!" I really
jumped that man an' he was gettin' pretty hot. But the next day he
cooled off an' you know, he raised both me an' Barney's wages
the next day.

Actually guidin' them dudes in the summertime ain't so great
'cause all you get at that time of year is stenographers an' teachers
an' all those kind'a people that's strictly on a budget. You jist don't
get much in tips then. You'd guide about ten of 'em an' maybe get
$2.50 or $4.00 in tips from the whole bunch. But in the spring or
fall when you got the regulars you'd average about $5.00 a day, or
$15.00 for a three-day trip. An' that was pretty good money in
those days, 'cause it wasn't very hard work.

There were sometimes I wouldn't get to bed 'til about four in
the morning. Probably been drinkin' all night. An' then I'd have
to be out there in the barn at five-thirty to clean stalls an' saddle
mules.

But when it came to going down the trail I'd take a bottle of
whiskey with me, an' heck, half the time I'd go to sleep ridin' that
mule down into the canyon.

Wranglin' dudes in the Grand Canyon, 1935

But Golly, She Was
an Awful Nice Ol' Gal

DUDE WRANGLIN' was quite a thing in my day. The reason you wrangled dudes was that you made more money, an' there always was a little somethin' on the side. Now a cowboy's a gentleman, an' all that stuff, you understand what I mean, but the fact is you was always lookin' around for a specially good-lookin' dude. You know what I mean—some gal you could be datin'.

Well, this one time up there at the Grand Canyon I had this lady and her son on a canyon trip. Golly, she was an awful nice ol' gal. I'd taken 'em down, an' when we got back I had a date with her. An' goldurn I jist decided I'd give her the big charge—heck, nothin' gained, nothin' lost. I wound up in her room, an' the last thing anybody wants to do is to get caught in a room of one of those big hotels with a dude gal, especially if you're workin' for the place.

Frankly, I didn't care, so I came down out of there about five o'clock that morning, an' all those desk clerks an' everybody saw me, an' I guess they told the boss. Well, I didn't care if they did fire me; I was gettin' kind'a tired of dudin' at the canyon anyway. I guess that gal kind'a learned about cowboyin' from me.

OO

An' there was that time about 1930 when I went to work for Jack Burden dudin' down there at Wickenburg, Arizona, at the Remuda Ranch. I got into a lot of trouble with ol' Jack. You see, I was doin' pretty well out there on the ranch. I was a cowboy singer and a good dude wrangler. I was breakin' horses an' gettin' along with the dudes fine. Always had an answer for everybody, you know. They really put up with a lot off me that they wouldn't have put up with from anybody else.

But you see, what happened was that I got into a fight with this dude over a goldurn dude girl. I was goin' with this girl an' we had quite a case on one another. She'd come out there for two years straight an' we had somethin' goin'. Then this dude guy, he got to kind'a tryin' to court her, an' one night I guess he'd taken her out somewhere an' that made me kind'a mad. I said what I shouldn't an' I stomped off to town an' got drunk.

Well, when I got back there they was just gettin' out of the car. I really charged that dude, an' I was really workin' him over when a batch of the hands jumped me an' locked me up in my little house down by the corral. They took me down there, put me to bed, you know, to sober up an' just locked me in that place. About daylight I busted out of the damned house, caught a little ol' sorrel horse, saddled up an' went across the river. Ol' Jack Burden was there on the other side in his car an' met me at the bridge. He says, "Well, if you're gonna stay drunk, you're gonna have to have some money, I guess."

I says, "I guess so."

He paid me off, an' I said, "I'll bring your horse back."

An' he said, "Oh hell, keep him. Nobody else wants to ride him anyway."

So I rode off, went over to a bootleggin' joint and stayed drunk the rest of the day. Never did know whether ol' Jack had fired me, or whether I quit.

FC

Talkin' about dudes, I just got to get this off my chest about them Hollywood cowboys. When I look at a television western these days I get disgusted. I don't know if you remember, but they used to have one called *Rawhide,* an' they was movin' a trail herd all the time, an' it showed pictures of all the cowboys around the fire. Now, what I want to know is, who in the hell was out there standin' guard on the cattle if all the cowboys was stayin' warm around the fire?

I never seen a western picture that was made to where it was really and truly what you would call the real cowboy life. Those pictures was just a lot of hooey.

Ol' John Wayne, the actor, is a great friend of mine. I worked on a picture with him one time, an' we was talkin' about how in all the western pictures that you ever saw, the cowboy rode only one horse. Well, actually you had a string of 'em, see? An' you never on those westerns saw anybody feedin' a horse. Nobody's ever feedin' a horse. The same durn way with the shootin'. They shot an' shot an' never reloaded their six-shooters—just kept on shootin'. Like, I was talkin' with John Wayne when they was makin' this picture *Helldorado* down at Old Tucson. We was out there talkin', an' they had all these horses tied up to the hitchin' rail. An' golly, every time a horse had an off-fall, you know what I mean, somebody would run in there with a shovel an' a wheelbarrow to haul it off. So I said to John, I says, "Jiminy Christmas, that ain't natural. A horse tied up there half a day an' there ain't nothin' behind him."

John laughed, an' I says to him, "It jist ain't natural, but I guess it all comes out all right, 'cause you never see 'em feedin' the horses in the movies anyway."

+S

Now you got me talkin' about the movie days. I sure had a time when I went over to Hollywood in 1929. I'll tell you them was the days. I was workin' one time on that *Cimmaron* picture with Richard Dix up at Fresno, California, an' they was havin' a real big scene, a land rush. Golly, they had about fifteen hundred head of horses, an' lots of wagons an' buggies, an' they hired everybody in the world—a lot of guys who couldn't even ride a horse.

We had these wagons all set up out there to make this one big scene, an' that goldurn sun wouldn't come out. So we sat there for three days, settin' in them wagons, drinkin' whiskey, playin' poker an' shootin' craps all day. Jist waitin', waitin' for the sun, but gettin' paid all the time.

An' then we came back to Hollywood to make some other scenes out at the RKO Ranch, an' this friend of mine who lived up at Saugus, old Andy Jauregui, had these oxen an' wagons an' mule teams. We was drinkin' pretty heavy. Well, I borrowed one of those bullwhips, one of those big, long bullwhips, an' I was poppin' it, showin' my friends how to make 'em pop. Damned if I didn't stampede a mule team an' wreck a scene, an' that made the director madder than hell.

"Get out, you drunkards," he hollered, an' fired the bunch of us.

6

There was a lot of funny incidents from those movie days. I don't know whether I ought to mention names, but there was a little actress, an English comedienne, by the name of Daphne Pollard. An' out there at Pathé they was makin' a wild west movie, an' bein' I was a bronc rider an' what, they wanted me to work in it. It was kind'a like a wild west show, a comedy with this little English girl starrin'. She wore those ol' hightop shoes with elastic on the sides, wore funny hats an' everythin' else. She was just comical as hell.

Well, my job was to ride those buckin' horses, an' one day after I was finished ridin', why I was settin' up in the grandstand with another feller an' all of a sudden here comes this Daphne Pollard, an' she looked over at me an' said, "You know, you look jist like my brother over in England."

An' I said, "Yeah, I do?"

She looks at me an' says, "By golly, you'd sure make a double for him."

Well, we got kind'a friendly, an' I noticed she always carried a big ol' heavy coat on her arm, had it with her every time she wasn't in a scene. We was settin' there talkin' when they called her to come out an' shoot a scene. They kept hollerin' for her an' pretty soon she got up, pulled a fifth of whiskey out from under her coat an' said, "Here, take care of this for me 'til I get back an' then we'll all have a drink."

This other guy an' me, we had a coupla big snorts an' then she comes back an' had a couple snorts, too, an', aw heck, we got kind'a half tight on that bottle of whiskey. An' goldurn if she didn't bring a bottle back to the set each day. Now, I don't know how she come to pick me. Maybe alcoholics just look alike. I don't know whatever happened to her.

This movie stuff can get pretty rough at times, you better believe me. Like the time they was making this sequel to *Beau Geste*. I think it was RKO or Paramount, I forget which it was. But, anyway, they had this fort, you know, like they have in Morocco, for—what do you call those guys?—yeh, the foreign legion. But this wasn't the foreign legion that I was a-workin' with; it was a bunch of A-rabs—A-rab cavalrymen, see.

There was a bunch of us, golly, they was quite a bunch of us—thirty or forty on horseback—an' we all had these turbans on our heads, long coats, an' sabres, an' rifles, you know, an' ridin' these durned Arabian saddles. And we was attackin' this fort where this foreign legion was.

Frank awaits the next bronc in this 1939 photograph

An' here was these soldiers up in the fort an' down on the ground, a-firin' an' shootin', an' the bunch of us A-rabs, renegade A-rabs. Well, we was supposed to charge through this big arch they had built an' charge right over these guys on the ground. Some of 'em was supposed to be shot an' die.

Well, we had a couple rehearsals an' goldurn these guys shootin' up at us from the ground was shootin' blanks, but they was shootin' up in our faces an' three or four of us got powder burns. We hollered about that, an' the next day when we got ready for that scene some of us had been drinkin' an' we said, we'll fix those guys this time.

By golly, when we was supposed to charge 'em again, goldurn if we didn't just run right over 'em. Heck, we put about six of 'em in the hospital. An' that wasn't even the take, either; it was jist another rehearsal. Believe me, when we did make the big shot, there wasn't anybody shot off a gun in our faces.

An' that wasn't all of it. There was this one scene where the head of the cavalry was supposed to stop in front an' wave his pistol for his men to follow him. Actually, it was the actor's double who was on that horse. Well, before they shoot a great big scene like that they always put the si-rene on. Like for a small scene, they jist holler, "Silence," but for a big picture they put the si-rene on— like for when you have a charge or somethin'.

An' these ol' picture horses, they'd been in so many of these pictures, the minute they heard this si-rene they was ready to go. Well, here was this double on this horse, an' he had kind'a stopped there, an' this ol' horse I had, the minute he heard the si-rene he was off chargin' an' I couldn't stop him no way, shape or form. That ol' boy in front of me turned his horse an' I guess I hit him broadside. Goldurn if that didn't turn me an' him and both horses right over. Didn't hurt any of us, but I don't know how it didn't kill us. That was the closest I ever come to gettin' hurt in a movie.

Used to do some packin' for the movies, too. One time we was up at Lake Tahoe, an' they were making the picture called *Rose Marie* with Jeannette MacDonald an' Nelson Eddy in 1935.

Remember when they was singin' that *Indian Love Call* to each other way up in the mountains? Well, I was the guy that packed that organ—packed it on a mule—an' took it up there on the mountain for that movie. In the picture they only showed them singin' for a couple of minutes, but we was settin' around an' listenin' to them two singin' that *Indian Love Call* all day.

There was several of us doin' the packin' up there, me an' my friend Bill Chick an' a couple of more guys. Bill was a bronc rider an' we had made some rodeos together. Well, in this picture they had a big drum an' Indians dancin' on it. An' they had another bunch of Indians who were supposed to ride a bunch of pinto horses in a circle around the drum.

The Indians were ridin' bareback, an' that was all right. But, you see, they had picked up all the pintos they could find in the area, an' a lot of them were broncs. Well, durin' the rehearsals those pintos was a-buckin' all those Indians off. It was sure a big mess.

So Bill Chick an' I took those pintos over an' broke all of 'em to ride bareback. We did it in about two days, an' we were about half drunk all the time, but goldurn if we didn't break those pintos an' get them to runnin' around that durn drum. We sure had a lot of fun them two days. Ol' Yakima Canutt, who was an old-time bronc rider, was the head stunt man and stunt director on the picture.

You Can Get Used
to S-s-s-stutterin'

NOW A LOT OF PEOPLE'S been curious about my stutterin' an' how I could be an entertainer. Well, I'd like to tell you about that. One time a feller an' me even had an act that included stutterin'. This guy, his name was Sam Fenner, would be up there on the stage an' he would say to the audience, "Now, who out there would like to come up here an' join me in a song?"

Well, I'd be settin' there in the crowd, an' I'd wait awhile an' then I'd raise my hand an' stand up. I'd say, "I'd sure like to come up there an' s-s-s-sing with you."

That guy would jist break out laughin' an' say, "How are you gonna come up here an' sing with the way you s-s-s-stutter?" He was jist a-funnin' me for the crowd.

Well, I'd jist go up there to the stage an' sing away as sweet a-singin' as you could hear. An' there wasn't any stutterin'. You see, you jist don't stutter when you sing.

An' there was this time I was takin' these horses up north for ol' Doc Pardee. I was about eighteen or nineteen then. I was headin' for the Fox Barrows private school south of Flag, an' I stopped overnight at Cornville where this big ol' boy was workin' a farm. Ol' Doc Pardee knew this guy stuttered an' he figured they was settin' me up for a pretty good one.

I got up there to Cornville, an' this big feller—he was about 250 pounds—he was out there in the fields ridin' a-top a disc or a plow, I forget which. So I rode over to the fence an' at that time in my life it happened that I st-st-st-stuttered awful bad, you know. But I didn't pay much attention to it. I may have had trouble talkin', but I talked. I always had s-s-s-somethin' to s-s-s-say an' I'd s-s-s-say it.

Well, I rode over to that fence an' I hadn't said a word. It just happened he talked first.

An' that guy st-st-st-stuttered worse than I did. I mean he was a st-st-st-stutterin' son of a gun.

He was kind'a gettin' red-faced, so I told him right off, "Listen, I st-st-st-stutter, too. I st-st-st-stutter a helluva lot."

Well, I don't know what it is, but an awful lot of stutterin' people like to talk, an' this ol' boy hadn't seen nobody for quite some time, I guess, an' so we talked there all that evenin'. He cooked supper, an' golly, he wanted to talk an' wanted to talk. An' both of us were a-talkin', an' both of us was a-stutterin'. An' damn it, if we didn't get to stutterin' worse than we had before. An' you know, we set up talkin' 'til twelve o'clock that night. It was the damnedest conversation you ever heard. I often thought if they'd had tape recorders in those days an' somebody'd taped that stutterin' conversation, well, it'd been worth a million dollars.

An' don't you think when I got up to the school, ol' Doc and the people at the school thought they'd really set me up. Why, they couldn't wait to ask me, "How did you make out down there at Cornville with that ol' boy?"

I didn't let on anythin' at first. I jist said, "Fine. Got along jist fine." I wouldn't let on a thing had happened an' those guys was just dyin' to find out how those two stutterin' fools had got along. I strung 'em out an' then told the story jist like I told you.

A Cowboy's Paradise

YOU KNOW, this dudin' could be awfully rewardin'. Like the time I was workin' up at this place at Lake Tahoe in California, an' I seen this ol' gal unloadin' her stuff out of her car. (She was the same gal I got fired over at the Grand Canyon.) It wasn't long before I was her private guide an', golly, we had quite a little set-to up there. She was built awful good, an' she was married an' there was this funny little thing that happened. I don't know whether it wants to get printed, but I'll tell you the story anyway.

That ol' gal liked ridin' up in the mountains by the lakes, an' one day we was up there an', damn, if we didn't make drinks out of her scotch and the snow that was on the ground in patches. We was gettin' along jist fine when she pulls out a movie camera an' hands it to me. An' she says to me, "You know, my husband would sure like to get some movies of me runnin' naked in the forest."

Of course, I was surprised for a minute or two, but I grabbed that camera an' she shucked her clothes. An' pretty soon, there I was up there in the mountains takin' movie pictures while she was runnin' naked as a jaybird through an' around those goldurn pine trees!

$\mathcal{G}$

You got to figger after a little incident like that you're still kind'a friendly with the ol' gal, an' I guess I just moved up in her room in the hotel. That didn't set real well with the hotel people, an' one night the wrangler boss calls the room an' says, "You better get your ass out of there. The manager says if you don't get out, he's gonna send all the security officers up there an' take you out."

Well, you don't have to shove me too hard to get me to understand a situation. I got out of there an' went down to Reno, Nevada. That was the first time I was down there, an' I want to tell you it was a cowboy's paradise there in 1935. I'm not kiddin' you, that was a cowboy's paradise, 'cause when I hit Reno that's when the divorcées was really startin' to come in there.

So I went to wranglin' dudes out at those little ranches where these divorcées would come to stay while all the legal procedures

was goin' through. I went to work out there at a riding stable. I really got to funnin' around. Those gals, they wanted to take you out on parties, you know, drinkin' parties. An' heck, you didn't have to have any money; they had plenty of money. An' they'd slip twenty-five or thirty dollars in your pocket to pay for drinks an' everythin'.

I was a pretty good dancer, an' I had a pretty good line. So I got to be quite a gigolo for a little while up there. I'd get awful drunk an' finally I jist quit that job up there. I said, "Hell, there ain't no use of me workin'." So I married up with this woman, Patty Cottchalk, an' we moved into a hotel an' stayed there for a while.

But you know how it is with an ol' cowboy who never had too much—you give him a big, ol' car to drive an' a pocketful of money, goldurn, he goes crazy.

This gal wasn't too wealthy, but she had quite a little money, an' this was my first marriage—1935 an' '36. We went on down to Phoenix, an' I was ridin' in the rodeos, makin' quite a few shows, but I got to drinkin' awful bad. The truth is I was gettin' to where I was gettin' too drunk, an' I would ride a horse for about six seconds an' just give plum out. So I said, "Hell, to hell with it."

So we went over to Hollywood an' she bought an apartment house an' I started workin' in pictures. I worked in pictures an' got drunk, an' then she'd get to drinkin' awful heavy, too. Well, there was this time—there was this incident, you see, I'd taken the cure an' quit drinkin' entirely, but she hadn't. There was a guy up in the apartment above us an' he was an illustrator, illustratin' some children's books, but his hobby was wood carvin'. His name was George Mitchell, that was his name, an' he'd sit out on the steps of his apartment just whittlin' away. An' that's how I kinda got started whittlin' just to pass the time away. You see, I got to where I couldn't work. I'd quit drinkin', you know, but I got kind'a sick. Actually, I was supposed to have a lung infection—that's what the doctor said. But that's what got me started carvin'.

This ol' friend of mine, Tex Wheeler, the sculptor, was stayin' down at the home of that great western cartoonist, J. R. Williams, down in Santa Monica Canyon, right across from the Will Rogers Ranch. An' ol' Tex was helpin' me out, showin' me about carvin' an' modelin'. One day—it was Patty's birthday—Tex had me come out to watch him work buildin' a model. So I said to Tex, "Tex, this is her birthday. We'll go on back into town an' have a little party."

Well, goldurn it, we came back into town there, an' there she was drunker 'n a skunk, all regards to her. An' she is in the bathtub a-takin' a bath an' couldn't get out of the tub. So I got her out of the bathtub an' went down an' got some beer an' whiskey. I was pretty aggravated an' I jist got drunk as a skunk. Ol' Tex got a girl friend of his up there an' we partied. We got drunk, all of us, an' we partied for two days. Before ol' Tex left he invited us to come on out to his place for a barbecue. I had sobered up an' I didn't want to go. My wife wanted to go an' I didn't. Well, she up an' pulled out a little suitcase with bathin' suits an' goldurn it, five pints of whiskey.

She called a taxicab, an' when that cabbie came to the door I just run him off. I said, "I ain't goin' no place. I'm goin' to stay

right here." Durn if this taxicab driver didn't come back pretty soon, an' so I said, "Hell, give me a pint of whiskey." An' then we both got in the taxi an' headed for Tex's place.

I had a dog then, a pretty good little dog, an' I took him with me in that taxi. My wife an' I got in some kind of argument, an' here that cab is goin' out Sunset Boulevard right out to Santa Monica Canyon, an' damn, if right in the middle of that argument she didn't jist throw my dog out the taxicab window!

So, goldurn it, I hollered at that cabbie to stop, an' I got the dog back in there. I was pretty mad an' I must have hung one on her, or somethin', an' she said to the cabbie, "Stop an' let me out of here."

An' I can still remember hearin' him say, "If you want out, lady, jist jump out." I guess he was gettin' kind'a tired of our fightin' an' wanted to get us out to where we was goin'.

Well, by golly, Patty jumped out of that cab an' busted her head open. They had pictures of it in those Los Angeles papers afterwards. You see, when the cab stopped, why there was police an' photographers right in back of us. An' I guess I got sore an' really hung one on one of the cops. They had me handcuffed to the doggone car an' everythin'.

I couldn't figure out how those cops an' reporters had got there so fast until I found out the cabbie had called them an' told them there was a heck of a story about these two drunks who were fightin' an' he was goin' back to pick them up.

Well, they made a pretty good splash of it in the L.A. papers, an' because of that incident her an' I busted up.

∩

After that I wandered around. Went down to Tucson, had a wood-carvin' place there, but just kept gettin' drunk. An' then I went up north an' landed at Kanab in Utah where they was shootin' a movie with this Wild Bill Elliott. Didn't get a job with them, but I stayed around. An' then another movie outfit came in to shoot *Drums along the Mohawk* with Henry Fonda an' Claudette

Colbert. An' I got a job as one of the soldiers in that goldurn movie.

That's Mormon country up there, strictly Mormon country, an' durn if I didn't get drunk with a bunch of them Mormons. I guess there was ten of us that got drunk, but, you know, I was the only one, the only one, that got throwed in jail.

3A

Well, it wasn't long before I got on back to Reno an' went to work out at those dude ranches where the divorcées came. I knocked around a bit, did some dudin' an' some wood carvin', an' then my ol' friend, Barney Iles, you know, the one that was the entertainer up at the Grand Canyon, wanted me to come out to stay at this Valley Ranch. Ol' Barney had married a divorcée in Reno an' then bought that ranch.

Golly, there was nothin' out there at that ranch but divorcées —an' I mean all kinds of them—an' they was drunk every night. They had a big bar out there, an' everybody would be partyin' an' gettin' drunk. When I was sober, I'd play the guitar an' sing—if I do say so myself, I could play the guitar an' sing fairly good. An' sometimes the drunker I got, the better I sang. An' I used to tell stories, too, I mean stories that was sometimes on the shady side. I was quite an entertainer in those days.

Well, this was about 1940, I guess, an' it was at that place that I met Joan Kaufman. She was there gettin' a divorce. She was quite a gal. She was from Marquette, Michigan, an' her father an' Al Smith built the Empire State Buildin'. An' there was eight children, an' every time her mother had a baby her father would give her a million dollars. An' they was called the "million dollar babies," all eight of 'em. An' all of 'em was alcoholics, I think, includin' Joan.

Now Joan was out there at that ranch gettin' a divorce. I don't know how many times she'd been married; one time she was married to one of those fancy Biddles from Philadelphia. But she was a good gal, honest; she was a heck of a good gal.

An' she'd come out to this ranch 'cause there was people in town, in Reno—what they called dude ranch brokers. They'd contact the divorcées, find a dude ranch for 'em to stay, or their lawyers'd contact them an' set up the place to stay. I guess those dude ranchers would kind'a pay off the lawyers an' the brokers—at least that's what Joan told me afterwards.

I didn't know at first that she drank quite a bit. In fact, I didn't pay no attention to it. But, by golly, we kind'a got together nicely out there at that ranch an' we had a little set-to.

Well, after she got her divorce, her an' I decided to get married. She quit drinkin', an', by golly, we had a big weddin'. Heck, everybody was there. We had the weddin' in town at a place they called the Roundup Bar. That was quite a place, there. Sometime back I'd carved the back bar there. The gal that owned that place paid me pretty good for doin' it but by the time I got it carved, I had drunk so much at that bar I still owed her money.

Anyhow, we had this big weddin' an' everybody came. There was reporters an' photographers 'cause Joan was quite a prominent gal, you know, society kind. Well, we moved into this little house down there on Liberty Street an' it wasn't long before we owed everyone in town. You see, we'd started drinkin', both of us, an' Joan's mother had cut her off, wasn't sendin' her a dime. I guess she was mad 'cause her socialite daughter had married one of them cowboys out in Reno.

I guess we stayed drunk two or three months, an' we owed everybody in the goldurn town. One day, why Joan goes downtown—see, we didn't even have a phone to use in our house—an' she called her mother up an' she tells her she needs some money. An' her mother says to her, "I'll tell you what I'll do. If you'll divorce that Frank Polk I'll contact a lawyer out there an' send enough money to pay all your bills—for everythin' you owe—an' buy you a ticket to New York (her mother was in New York then). I'll pay for the divorce, an' I'll give you some money, too."

So Joan, she come back an' told me about that. Well, you know, we was talkin' through alcohol; we was doin' that alcoholic thinkin'. You're not really bein' a crook or a thief, you just do those things 'cause it's jist your alcoholic thinkin'. So we started to get a plan in mind, an' Joan, she says to me, "I don't want to divorce you. Tell you what we'll do. We'll just go ahead an' get a divorce an' get all the bills paid by my mother. An' I'll get me a ticket on the airplane to New York that stops in Elko, Nevada."

"An' I get a ticket to Elko, Nevada, an' we'll get married again!"

Well, everythin' started workin' out. Her mother sent her lawyer in Reno some money an' he got all our bills paid off. I guess it was quite a bit for those days, about fifteen or sixteen hundred dollars, an' her mother told the lawyer to give my wife about five hundred dollars.

We got that divorce in the mornin' an' everyone came out to see Joan off at the airport. The lawyer was there, too, an' I went up to him an' said, "Would you mind if I got on the plane to tell her goodbye, kind'a private-like, you know . . . ?"

He didn't know I had bought me a ticket to Elko, an' he said, "I guess it's all right. I guess it's fine."

So I get on the airplane—an' don't get off. Stayed right on an' both of us got off at Elko an' got married the next mornin'. So there we were. Got all our bills paid off—an' this is your alcoholic thinkin'—got all our bills paid, got five hundred dollars in cash an' Joan cashes in the rest of her plane ticket which was another one hundred dollars. So we're back in business, see what I mean?

We came on back to Reno, stopped there for a day or so an' then she wanted to go down an' visit her uncle in Los Angeles, an' I had a bunch of wood carvin's that I was tryin' to sell. We stayed down there with her uncle, an' we still drank. An' we was still drinkin' when we got back to Reno. We just stayed drunk in this place I rented, an' then her mother called an' said, "You got to divorce him this time." So she came out to Reno this time, herself. She was gonna see that the divorce was done up proper this time.

If I was that kind'a guy I guess I could'a got a bundle out of that divorce. An' her mother was really scared it was goin' to cost her a lot of money. But I told her I wasn't lookin' for any money. We got a divorce an' parted as friends, real good friends.

But, golly, you can't believe what those papers—especially those Hearst papers in Los Angeles—did with that story of our gettin' a divorce an' then gettin' remarried right away. They just had a field day, played it up in those papers for a month or so.

I guess it was only six months that I was married to Joan, but she was a nice ol' gal. Really a nice ol' gal.

Now a lot of people are still askin' me about those days in Reno. Why just the other night they had a movie on the late, late show on TV. It was a movie with Gary Cooper in *The Cowboy and the Lady,* an' it was about those cowboys an' those gay divorcées in Reno. Some people say the guy who wrote that movie had got the idea from those newspaper stories about Joan an' me.

What brought those women out to Reno was a law they passed in the early thirties where you could be a six-week resident an' get a divorce. An', golly, there was a lot of those eastern gals comin' out to Reno to get divorced. A lot of those ol' gals was pretty good ol' gals. A lot of 'em had never stepped out on their husbands, but their husbands was steppin' out on 'em.

I'd gone out with a lot of those divorcées when I was dudin' up there, an' they'd get a little drunk an' several of 'em would tell me they hadn't slept with their husbands for five years.

It was kind'a interestin', the way these ol' gals came out there. You see, they had to have a witness who'd say they was in Reno for six weeks, an' they'd get that witness out there at the ranch.

Those women that came out to Nevada weren't like the dudes you wrangled at the guest ranches in Arizona. These were all kind'a disturbed women in a certain way; disturbed, you know, 'cause of the divorce troubles. An' a lot of 'em had never drunk much, or never stepped out. But when they came out to Reno, why it was the first time they'd ever run into a deal like this an' they kind'a went haywire.

I guess to them it was romantic seein' these cowboys, even if some of 'em were phonies, city guys livin' off the cowboy's reputation. An' I guess us cowboys were really livin' it up, too. Heck, out on the ranch you didn't dress anythin' special. But in Reno, everybody wore a big hat an' a pair of boots, an' you wore an awful lot of tailor-made shirts. You could get a shirt made over in San Francisco—there was a Chinaman over there by the name of Sing Kee, an' he would make you the best gabardine shirt you ever saw for six an' a half dollars.

An' there was one store there in Reno, called Parkers, owned by a Jew, an' he was a heck of a nice guy, an' those dude gals—an' dude men, too, 'cause they was comin' out for divorces, too—would go over there an' buy him out. They all wanted to wear some western clothes, you see. So you'd be runnin' the dudes over to this store, an', golly, they'd buy at that time maybe three or four hundred dollars worth of western clothes. Well, this guy that was runnin' the store, he'd take you in the back an' give you a big hat, or a coupla shirts, or a pair of pants, just for bringin' those people in.

An', as I was tellin' you before, those gals would give you, say, forty dollars or so to escort them around, an' the experienced guys, they'd tell you, put half of it in your pocket an' spend the rest on the lady.

Of course, the truth is that a lot of those cowboys were goin' out with those gals with expectations of marryin' a lot of money. An' there was a lot of 'em that did. Well, some of 'em did, an' some of 'em didn't. You take a guy that had a drinkin' problem that was an alcoholic problem, like me, why the thing jist wouldn't work out. An' that was really the problem with Joan an' me.

There was a lot that attracted us to each other at the beginnin'. I was a cowboy singer, sang songs an' played guitar, an' I entertained the dudes, an' I also had that wood-carvin' shop out there. Joan Kaufman, why she was just attracted to me, an' I was attracted to her.

Everythin' in the world was written about us, but, heck, a lot of it wasn't true. It was jist what a reporter thought he ought to write. Sure, Joan was rich, at least her family had a lot of money, an' she had been married to a Biddle. But she wasn't what you call main-line society. Really an' truly, she wasn't like that. She didn't like society; that wasn't her type of thing. Oh, I'll tell you that gal could talk French. She'd been educated, been sent to France to schools, an' she could play the piano like nobody's business. Had a lot of talent. She didn't like classical stuff; she liked to get down in those goldurn joints an' take over the piano an' play that boogie woogie. Really an' truly she didn't care much for this goldurned society stuff. Her family an' her mother was very much on the society stuff, though.

An' there was a lot of things between us. She liked music an' I liked music. She liked to dance an' I liked to dance. She liked to drink an' I drank. Really an' truly, she had an awful lot of good points. But she was alcoholic. Joan, she was rebellin' against the things her family wanted her to be.

An' after her mother got her to divorce me the last time, gol-durn if her mother didn't pick a guy for her. He was supposed to be the son of some high-falutin' guy, an' they was married quite a long time. But it didn't work out. I heard it cost Joan's mother $50,000 to get rid of that guy.

The Cure . . .
The First Time Around

SOME PEOPLE MIGHT SAY I shouldn't be talkin' so much, tellin' so many stories about when I was drinkin', but the truth is it's better to get it all out in the open.

One time, you know I ran into this ol' gal who'd been the drunkest, dirtiest gal I ever saw—why she'd jist been a mess. But this time, by golly, I saw her on the street an' she looked pretty good, looked really nice—all dressed up.

At this time I was down on my heels. I'd been drinkin' an' sick an' I asked her for some money to buy a bottle. She gave me the money an' then she said, "Have you ever thought of gettin' into AA?" You know, that's that Alcoholics Anonymous. I said no, but the fact is I was thinkin' about that ol' AA.

Anyhow, I took that gal's money, bought a bottle an' I got drunk. I really got sick, an' when I straightened up a bit, I went back an' talked to that gal, an' she called a guy from this goldurned AA. Well, they met in this place up over an ol' stable—this was in Reno—an' really an' truly I practically crawled up them steps. But AA helped me get back on my feet, an' I did a lot of talkin' at AA groups.

Well, I stayed sober for quite a long time. Got to carvin' again an' then I ran into this gal that was drinkin' an' I tried to get her sobered up. An' I did, an' we got married. Her name was Wanda, Wanda Remington, an' goldurn, if she wasn't an alcoholic. Seems all birds of a feather flock together. Anyhow, we stuck it out a long time together; we was married in 1948 an' stayed together for eighteen years.

I stayed sober an' didn't get into any trouble. At this time I was carvin' all these figures, big ones—Indians, prospectors, an' such—an' one-armed bandits, on those slot machines. I did well with those things; had three guys workin' for me an' bar owners was buyin' them for the bars up in Virginia City an' Elko, Nevada. We also rented them durn things out in Reno an' Las Vegas.

I was doin 'some western art at this time, but western art wasn't sellin' too good, so you had to do an awful lot of commercial stuff. That's when I got in with this outfit carvin' those one-armed bandits—full-size figures, you know. I was makin' a lot of money out of those things, but I was doin' a heckuva lot of gamblin', too. What's funny is that there's a lot of those figures still around. A

bunch of 'em has been sold to antique dealers in California an' there's about six of 'em down at that Saddleback Inn at Santa Ana.

Now, you see, there wasn't a lot excitin' about my life at this time, 'cause I wasn't drinkin'. That's funny, ain't it? The funny incidents that happened to me in my life was when I was a-drinkin'.

But I'll show you how easy it is to slip back. About 1959 we moved down to Prescott, an' one day when I got back from a trip, I found my horse had slipped out of a broken fence an' got killed deader than heck on the highway. I had to haul him off the road an' I was feelin' pretty bad. So I thought I'd just go an' get me a bottle of beer—you know, just to make me feel a little better. For an alcoholic, why that's all you have to do—take that one drink. An' damned if I didn't get on a drunk an' I stayed drunk about a week or two.

Well, when I sobered up I figured I had to get out of there, so the wife an' me, we moved down to Tucson an' I started carvin' manikins an' this cowboy that we put a-top a plastic horse. I carved them for Harold Porter for his store down in Tucson. Golly, that work just straightened me out. I'd stayed sober for eleven years, from 1948 till about '59. Then I took off again drinkin' when my horse was killed. But that job in Tucson straightened me out—I guess it was about 1960 or '61. That's when I finally straightened out an' I haven't had a drink since.

✝

It was about this time, too, that I got to sellin' my wood carvin's again, an' this great ol' friend of mine from Prescott, ol' George Phippen, got me interested in castin' my figures in bronze. An' it wasn't long before I was sellin' my first bronzes to that O'Brien's Art Emporium down in Scottsdale. My first bronze was a cowboy pullin' on a boot, changin' from an ol' pair of boots to a new pair, an' the ol' one had a hole in the sole.

I needed to sell those bronzes 'cause I was in terrible bad shape

Frank and one of his now-famous one-
armed bandit wood carvings in Reno, 1952

financially. Up there in Nevada in thirteen years, countin' the wood carvin's an' those one-armed bandits, I guess, heck, I must have made $90,000. But, you know, I left there with $2,000.

Finally, down there in Tucson I was makin' enough money on my art to buy a place, but things didn't work out. My wife, Wanda, she was drinkin' like a son of a gun an' I wasn't drinkin' at all. It wasn't workin' out an' so we divorced an' I paid her off in cash.

An', you know, it was sad. Wanda never straightened up. She was a-livin' in her car up around Vegas an' she died in her car. That's what happens to alcoholics. There's only three outs for alcoholics an' that's Alcoholics Anonymous, the insane asylum or the grave.

Romancin' with Mary

NOW I'D LIKE TO TELL YOU a little bit how I came to marry Mary, who's settin' here right by my side now. Used to know her back around Prescott. In fact, I hadn't seen her since 1943 when I was ridin' broncs at a rodeo there.

But I'm mixin' up my story a bit. You see, I was pullin' a horse trailer down through the Colorado mountains an' down into Farmington, New Mexico. That horse of mine was gettin' awful restless in that trailer an' I was lookin' for some place to unload him. I remembered one of my ol' friends, Bill Chick, was over there, an' I called him. Well, he set it up for my horse, an' then he said, "Say, do you know who is a-livin' here, an' she's all by herself? Mary Cooper Lackey, an' I bet she would sure like to see you."

Well, all I aimed to do was stay there a day with ol' Bill. But when Mary an' I got together, why we had a big party, danced all evenin'. We had a lot of fun for a couple of days an' then I headed back to Tucson. I thought it was all over. But I kept thinkin' about her. I would call her up an' then she'd call me an' we'd talk on the phone for an hour. An' pretty soon that damn phone bill was runnin' high as the sky.

To shorten things up a bit we made a date an' I drove to Gallup, New Mexico, met Mary there, an' we rode over to Albuquerque. An' we found out it was the real thing.

Well, Mary went back home an' I went home an' then we

started callin' up each other again. Finally, I said, "The only one thing to do is to get married, 'cause, golly, it was all right."

The only trouble was I didn't have any money; did kind'a poorly, you see, at the horse races in Albuquerque. But what I did was to take one of my bronzes over to Jack Goodman at the Mountain Oyster Club in Tucson. He sold it for me for $2,500, an' I sent Mary a check for $200, an' I called her an' said, "You get down here as quick as you can. You let me know when you get to Phoenix, an' I'll drive up an' 'meet you there."

Well, when we found out it took a wait of three days in Phoenix—heck, we weren't goin' to wait three days—why we took Mary's sister, Mattie, an' you know where we headed? We took Mattie along to be one of our witnesses an' we headed right up there for Vegas. Got married there the twenty-eighth of September, nineteen hundred an' seventy.

Frank and Mary Polk

Just Cowboyin'

WELL, THAT WAS MY ROMANCIN', an' if I say so myself, I wasn't a bad sort of lookin' guy when I was young. I'd like to get back to tellin' you about cowboyin', jist plain old cowboyin', you know, some little stories you might get a kick out of.

Like this friend of mine had been workin' the range where the cattle were wild, 'cause they hadn't worked that range for a spell. Well, this feller jumped a bunch of them wild cattle and he spotted the wildest goldurn heifer he ever saw. He decided that was the one he wanted to catch—he chased that damn thing all over the hills an' finally caught her.

Well, she didn't have an ear mark on her, but he could see a brand and he jist wondered what it was. Talk about your cowboy humor—there branded on her side in big ol' letters was "Oh Shit."

What probably happened was that some other guy must have run that thing for a long ways before he caught her an he was so mad, in place of branding her with the brand of the outfit he worked for, he just branded "Oh Shit" on her side. Never even bothered to ear mark her, just turned her loose.

Oh, there's a lot of cowboy namin' that's not too good to talk about certain places, but that was the way they talked out there. Now, you take an ol' wild mare a-runnin', when that mare is a-runnin', why she'll get to suckin' air in her rear end and the cowboys'll call her a "jill flirted mare." You see, cowboys have a certain kind of language of their own. They're all the time kiddin' and usin' expressions like nobody else.

They're a different breed today, either cowboyin' or rodeoin'. I'm not sayin' they are any better or worse. I know these kids ridin' the rodeos today is goldurn good, they are athletes. But I know one thing, they don't have the cowboy talk we had.

Now, there was the time when I was jist a kid—heck, I was only about eighteen—workin' for the Horseshoe outfit over in Bloody Basin, an' I was comin' down behind these pack mules. I was wranglin' mules to shoe some of them. An' whatever you was doin', you always had a hole in your rope, always had a loop built, 'cause if anythin' would break out you could ketch 'em quick. Well, there was this mule they called Tommy Arberry, a buckskin mule, one of the kitchen mules, an' he was just as gentle as he could be.

But, by golly, he jist didn't break out, but he kind'a dropped down one side of the trail, an' what I did, in place of hollerin' at him or goin' round him, I jist sailed a big ol 'skimmer out there an' roped him right around the neck. But I didn't jerk my slack up quick enough an' I jist caught him real deep back of the withers. I think he was about half asleep at the time, an' I mean he really came alive. I had my rope tied hard an' fast an', by golly, I knew that ol' mule would take straight off. So I jabbed the spurs into this damned brown horse—he was a bronc out of my rough string. An' when I jabbed my spurs into him, that ol' horse started buckin', an' here we come off that damned mountain—that pony a-buckin' an' that ol' mule down there on the end of my rope in front of me. He hit the end of that rope an' broke my back cinch. That left the back end of my saddle cocked up an' pretty soon that ol' mule hit the rope again an' jist jerked the saddle an' bridle right over this horse's head. An' I took the durndest fall—I practically rolled to the bottom of that doggone mountain.

An' I guess ol' Leonard Black, the cook, he heard the commotion an' came out there. I was knocked out cold an' he got some water an' poured it on me. When I came to, I looked up. There was the cook standin' over me. There was that ol' mule jist gazin' at me. An' that damned horse is standin' there, his front feet all tangled up in the front cinch, scared to move.

Me? I was skinned up from the top of my head to the tip of my toes. I mean I was the worst skinned-up person you ever did see.

OK

Let me tell you about another goldurn ol' horse that gave me jist a lot of trouble when I was workin' up there with the ol' Horseshoe outfit. There was an ol' cowboy by the name of Charlie Riles they had left up at the 6 Bars, workin' by himself. He was ketchin' and leadin' out wild cattle all by himself.

Ol' Charlie had been up there about six weeks or more by himself an' ketchin' these goldurn wild cattle. An' actually he already had quite a few in the holdin' pasture. So me an' the cook an' the pack outfit an' some other cowboys rode up there to this ol' rock house that was kind'a dug out of the rock and the roof had fell in. Charlie hadn't shaved for about six weeks an', by golly, did he have a set of whiskers! I'll never forget lookin' at him when we rode up to his camp. He was settin' there puttin' on his boots, an' his socks was all plumb wore out, an' he had a couple of ol' flour sacks he was wrappin' around his feet for socks. It was the darndest-lookin' outfit I ever saw.

Well, ol' Charlie says, "I heard you all was comin', so I cooked up some chuck for you."

Here we were, eighteen or twenty of us cowboys who was jist movin' camp to the 6 Bars to work that country. We was mighty hungry, but you know what ol' Charlie had cooked up? Why, all he had was a little pot of beans an' a little dried fruit. That's all he had cooked up. He was plumb out of chuck.

3

I had one of the goldurndest ol' horses in my string that you ever saw. He was never too bad to buck in the mornin', but he was a horse you had to watch quite a bit of the time. If he ever'd get you in a tight place, why he'd really throw it at you; he was jist kind'a waitin' for the right time.

I remember one day we was workin' out east of camp an' there was six or seven of us on this holdup. They was bringin' cattle down this canyon into the holdup, an' a damned ol' cow broke out. I caught her jist as quick as I could an' tied her down. I jumped back on this ol' horse 'cause I heard the cattle comin' an' I knew I had to get back to help turn the cattle 'cause we were liable to lose the whole bunch, you see? So we got these cattle into the holdup. An' everybody was a-tryin' to keep them from goin' through but there was quite a few that went on through, but they was caught an' tied down. It took an hour or so to get things all back together again.

Well, I told Bill Ryan, who was runnin' things, that I had an ol' cow that had broke out tied down up there. He sent a coupl'a guys with me to help bring her in, but when we got up there to where I'd tied her down, the ol' cow wasn't there. She was gone. So I rode out an' looked over the rim, an' here this ol' cow had rolled off the rim an' down in this damned brush. An' she's layin' down there with her feet jist stickin' right up in the air, see? So I thought, I'll go down there an' put my rope on her hind feet an' kind'a turn her over an' drag her on down to where one of these guys can put his rope on her horns an' lead her back in.

So I went down there an' put my rope on this ol' cow's hind feet an' started through the brush to turn her over. But when I came through the brush, why that big ol' horse figured this was the time to let me have it, an' I mean he really fell apart. That horse started buckin' an' I was tryin' to get that rope off the saddle horn.

That ol' horse kept buckin', an' in some way that damned rope had got down around my back an' down between the horse's hind legs, an' there I was jist tied onto that saddle. I knew I had to get the rope off the horn, an' here he was a-buckin' all over this damned hillside an' me tryin' to get the horn knot off my saddle horn.

Well, every time I tried to get the rope off that ol' horse would hit the ground an' I'd jist grunt. I was a prisoner of that damned rope. An' those other cowboys, why, they jist sat up there on the rim a-laughin' like crazy. They kept laughin' while that goldurn horse had me a-tied to my own saddle.

I finally got that rope off an' we got that ol' cow. But, man, I was really in a storm that day. Those guys thought it was funny, an' I guess it was to them a-settin' up there on the rim. But, why, you know, I could have got killed.

ʋP

Now, if you think I wasn't mad at that horse, you should have heard me cussin' him later that same day.

You see, later there was a steer that broke out, an' he broke out on my side. That winter it had snowed a lot and the snow had bent the brush down over the ditches, kind'a so you couldn't see where them ditches was.

Well, I was about to ketch this big steer, an' he went plumb out of sight, jist disappeared. He dropped down in this ditch an' goldurn, I couldn't stop this horse or nothin', an' this horse was right in the ditch on top of that steer. Well, another guy saw what happened, and they stopped the holdup. One of 'em caught the steer an' I got this ol' horse straightened up an' got out of there. We got back to the holdin' pasture, an' I want to tell you I was pretty aggravated with this ol' horse. Why, I could've got killed fallin' in there a-top that big steer. Yes, sir, I was a little aggravated with him. Twice in the same day he pretty near killed me.

When we got to camp I pulled the saddle off him an' I said to the boss, "That's the last time I'm goin' to put my saddle on that damned horse. He pretty near killed me twice today an' I'll be damned if I want to give him another chance. The damned horse ain't no good anyway. Even if he was a gentle horse, he ain't no damn good."

The boss said, "All right, you don't have to ride him." An' that horse was never rode no more, at least not that I know of.

ED

There was some days you jist couldn't win. Like that time that Neal Ryan had this cow caught up there on a bluff. The cow had broke out of the holdup, an' damned if that cow didn't go over a bluff an' jerked that Neal an' his horse right with her. That whole damn outfit landed on top of this bed of cholla cactus.

Well, I'll tell you that ol' boy looked jist like a pin cushion. The best thing to do was to get him an' his horse down to the river. Those damn needles will swell up an' come out when they get wet. Well, we picked cholla needles out of ol' Neal for days.

But it was that same day when ol' Elsa Brown was turnin' a bunch of cattle into this holdup an' he run into a mesquite limb. He hit that limb an' it didn't break off with him. Elsa jist kept a-goin' an' turned those cattle in. That evenin' in camp, well, ol' Elsa, he jist got to hurtin' awfully bad an' spittin' up blood. We was camped about forty miles out from the Horseshoe Ranch where the closest car was we could get to. So we decided we'd get him out of there that night. We put him on a horse an' we rode with him all night an' practically half the next day.

Ol' Elsa had broken his ribs an' one of 'em had splintered an' poked into his lungs. That was why he was spittin' up blood. That ol' boy was in the hospital for six months.

But he was a tough ol' boy, that Elsa. One time he was workin' at the Club Ranch by himself an' broke a leg. Why, he jist got up on his horse an' rode down to the Verde where he had his truck, an' damn if he didn't get in that truck with that broken leg an' all, an' drive himself down to the hospital in Phoenix.

ℕ

I don't know if you've actually ever been on a trail drive, but, you know, when they're on the move there's always one steer that gets a little hot, an', by golly, all the rest of the steers—an' I don't know why it is—they just start ridin' him. They'll just get to ridin' him. There'll be four or five steers just ridin' that same steer all the time. An', heck, if you don't cut him out, why he'll just get down on you. So if you're on a long drive, why they'll just cut him out.

They cut him out, an' pretty soon you've got another, an' another, an' pretty soon you'll have quite a bunch of steers that you drop back to trailin' behind the herd. What they called that little bunch is the "Sweetass Bunch." That's what they called 'em on account of these steers ridin' 'em, you know. So that's the name for 'em—the "Sweetass Bunch."

HK

There's a funny thing about stampedin' cattle. They'll run, you know, jist when they're the quietest, when they have laid down. An' it's strange, but they can be facing any way in the world, but when they get up they're all facin' the same way! Now that might sound strange to you, but it's really an' truly what happens.

An' that's really where their power comes from. Like there was this time we must have had about three hundred head of cattle in this adobe corral. An' goldurn if they didn't stampede an' break out of there, jist tore out the whole side of that adobe corral, an' the bottom of them walls was about four feet thick. You can see what force they have.

There was another little incident I want to tell you about. It was about the time we was bringin' in these cattle for shippin' an' we had these cattle in a trap. The trap is what they call a kind'a small holdin' pasture. Well, we ate an' was settin' round tellin' a bunch of western stories, an' got about half-tight. Then all of us scattered out an' made our beds down in different places around the trap. We tied up our horses and scattered out hay for them. Nobody was standing guard, and some of us who had got pretty drunk jist tied our horses to the fence. We left 'em saddled in case the cattle did run.

Ol' Curly Gray said to us, "Ain't you scared to sleep in those damned places? If those cattle run, they're goin' to come right down over the top of you." An' Guy Parker said, "Me? I ain't scared. Hell no, all I got to do is throw this ol' bed tarp up in their faces an' they'll jist scatter out around me."

So, we went to sleep an' along to mornin' we heard them cattle hit that goldurned fence an' the wires was singin'. An' them cattle was comin' right down towards us, straight towards us. An' man, we got out of those beds an' tried to get out of the way. Those horses that was tied to the fence broke loose in the panic. Well, we was lucky; we got out of the way an' them cattle jist came right by us. It was dark an 'there was nothin' we could do about 'em, nothin' to do in the world but to go back to bed, an 'wait 'til daylight.

Ol' Guy started back to his bed an' he had one boot on an' one boot off an' he couldn't find the missin' goldurn boot. "What in the world happened?" he said out loud.

Well, he had pulled his damned boots off, I guess, before he went to bed that night. You see, a cowboy, the first thing he puts on is his hat an' his boots. I don't think he'd ever pulled off his pants.

Well, the next mornin' when it was light enough to see, we got up an' started out lookin' for Guy's boot. An' we found it about fifty yards or so away, layin' up there in the wash. An' we figured out what he did. He had put on one boot, see, an' he couldn't get the other on in time when them cattle came chargin' down on him. We figured he put on one boot an' he had the other one in his hand an' ran—he was the first to run—up this wash where he dropped the goldurned boot. So we kidded him about it. We said he was usin' that boot for a quirt, you know. He was a-quirtin' himself with that goldurn boot, whippin' himself while he was runnin' plumb scared in front of those cattle. We had quite a time gettin' them cattle gathered that day.

O–O

When we was trailin' cattle to Glendale to ship we jist had one truck, an' they couldn't haul too many beds 'cause they had

that truck loaded with the cook outfit an' chuck. So two cowboys sometimes would use the same bed. A lot of times Bill Ryan, the owner of the outfit, would leave his bed up at the Verde an' use my bed on the trail drive to Glendale.

Now, I didn't mind him sharin' the goldurn bed with me. But that Bill, that dirty ol' son of a gun, would go to bed with his boots an' his spurs an' everythin' on. He was sleepin' an' holdin' his horse's reins in his goldurn hand, in case the cattle ran. Everybody else tied their horses close to their bed where they could get to 'em easy. Bill Ryan was the only one who slept with his horse's reins in his hand. I guess he thought 'cause he was the boss he had to be the first on his horse if the cattle ran.

I'll tell you, I couldn't sleep 'cause Bill's goldurn ol' horse was right there stompin' at the head of my bed. An' that Bill? Why durn if he didn't just sleep on like he was a log.

+U

Talk about bein' cold out there a-workin'. Why, I remember the time ol' Whistle Mills was kind'a the wagon boss of an outfit up north, the Oro's. The Oro Ranch was about sixty miles south of Seligman, Arizona. They had to trail a bunch of Mexican steers from Oro's to Seligman to ship, an' ol' Whistle asked me to help 'em. I'd been drunk in town for about a week, but I said, "Sure, hell, I'll go on out there with you."

But here it was dead in the wintertime, an' I don't think I even had a coat, maybe only a light jacket. I didn't even have a bedroll or anythin', but I went on out there with 'em. Ol' Whistle wanted me to drive that chuck wagon an' cook for the outfit. Well, when we got out there to their camp it was about two or three o'clock in the mornin' an' it was damn cold, so I jist crawled right into that bed with ol' Whistle.

The next mornin' Bill Sharp brought me a bedroll, an' he had one of those Mexican serapes to wrap around my shoulders. I mean this was right in the wintertime an' colder than a dirty son of a gun out there. I didn't want to cook, so I traded jobs with one of the guys and we started out to Seligman with this bunch of steers an' it started snowin' an' really turned cold. An' that ol' Whistle, he put me up on the point, right up on the point, you know, a-pointin' those steers.

Now there's no way bein' up there in front you could get off your horse. You had to stay on your horse all the time to slow those leaders—you had to keep those cattle pointed. But the guys that was ridin' flanks—on the sides—an' the drags, why they could get off an' walk once in a while an' warm up.

So I was up there on the point an' I had this serape wrapped around me jist like a goldurn ol' Mexican. Well, I'll tell you I sobered up in that cold—an' stayed sobered up. I think we was about five days goin' into Seligman with those damned steers, an' golly, I was pretty hostile to that ol' Whistle for puttin' me on the point. I figured out that he had figured that was the place for me— up there on the point where I'd get sobered up.

I'd worked with that ol' Whistle when I first went to work for the Yolo's, when I was a kid. But after that winter I guess I've cussed out ol' Whistle a thousand times.

The Gold Dust Twins

NOW YOU'VE HEARD ME TALK about my old buddy, Dave Hill, an' how we hung around together so much they called us the Gold Dust Twins.

Well, I'd kind'a like to tell you a little about us. This here particular story is about the time we was in Prescott, Arizona, an' heard they were havin' quite a show over at Payson. Dave an' I was always broke. We didn't have a car, so if we wanted to go to some ol' rodeo why we'd have to get a ride. An' there was this kid around Prescott, Sharkey Andres, a pretty smart kid, but he was the most comical thing you ever saw. He had a great big ol', thick glasses an' a big beak, an' he looked a lot like a bird.

One night we went to him an' said we was wantin' to go to Payson, an' he said, "Heck, I'd like to go up there with you." He had an ol' Model A Ford coupé, so we all started out. Now this was sometime back in the thirties, an' you went over through Camp Verde an' you had to ford the river; there wasn't no bridge there at that time. You forded the Verde, an' then you went up this ol' Strawberry Hill to Pine an' on to Payson. We stopped at Camp Verde an' picked up an ol' barber friend of ours by the name of Skeeter Tompkins, who wanted to go with us. An' ol' Skeeter had a gallon of whiskey, an' that pleased us fine about takin' him along.

So here we was the four of us in the one seat of this Ford coupé an' a-goin' up this hill to the show at Payson. We was goin' up this hill an' we was all drunk, an' goldurn if we didn't hit a cow goin' up there. Hell, we didn't even stop. That ol' cow, we just rolled her off an' we kept a-drivin' that damned Ford. The radiator was all caved in, but we kept drivin' until she really started steamin'. I guess we just burnt the damned engine up.

Well, there was this ol' cabin on the side of the road, so we just pushed the car off the road an' we went into that cabin. We drank some more whiskey an' then laid down to sleep in our bedrolls. This partner of mine, Dave Hill, he had a mania all the time for hidin' money when he had it. He was always thinkin' that somebody was tryin' to roll him. I don't know where he got that from, but even when we was stayin' in rooms at rodeos, he always hid his money somewheres. An' then when he'd sober up he'd have a helluva time findin' it.

This time we had twenty-six dollars between us an' Dave happened to have it on him. I never thought anythin' about that money until I woke up in the mornin' an' I walked out of the cabin an' there was that goldurn ol' Dave a-kickin' rocks all over the place. An' I mean, he was kickin' them this way an' that way, an' there was a jillion rocks over that goldurn ground. I looked at Dave an 'I said, "Dave, what in the hell are you doin'?"

An' he says to me, "You know, I hid that money under a rock out here somewheres an' I'm trying to find the rock."

Well, there was a jillion rocks there, I swear, an' we never did find that money.

Anyhow, the mailman came by an' he took us on into Payson for the show. Dave an' me, we was flat broke, but we wasn't worried. We knew we could always get some money to eat on, an' we could get some money to drink on. An' we always knew somebody who would pay our entry fees for the rodeo. But this kid that had driven his old Ford up the hill didn't have a cent an' he didn't know anyone.

Well, we camped out about three-quarters of a mile from Payson. It's up in that Apache country where they've got lots of acorns. Dave an' me, we had gone into town an' left Sharkey in camp drunk, an' when we came back to the camp, why, there was a sight I'll never forget. There, down on his hands an' knees, was this kid, a-gatherin' acorns as fast as he could an' eatin' 'em as fast as he could. An' those eyes behind them big ol' glasses was just a rollin' around. That was the comicalist-lookin' sight I ever saw.

Now jist the other day a reporter called from that paper over there at Payson, an' he said he was writin' somethin' for the annual rodeo edition. He said he wanted to write somethin' about the time four of us guys actually hanged a guy over there at the Payson rodeo.

Well, that really broke me up, 'cause that never happened. What did happen was that we was funnin' around an' we'd put a noose on Dave Hill's neck an' kind'a strung him up. Why, when we let him down he was only a little bit purple in the face. Ain't it somethin' the way stories will get stretched out!

An' that reminds me of another story about ol' Tex Wheeler, the artist, an' Dave Hill an' myself when we was together on a drunk in Prescott.

We was settin' out there at Granite Dells a-drinkin' away an' they decided they wanted me to sing. Well, I was drunk an' ornery an' I didn't want to sing. They kept askin' an' pretty soon I got mad an' sailed my damned guitar out into the lake. Well, durned if ol' Tex didn't wade out there and bring it back.

Later on we came on back to Prescott to the whorehouse at the Mason. Tex was the only one who had any money an' he stayed all night in this room with a gal. The next mornin' his clothes and his boots was still all wet from wadin' out into the lake. Well, he got his pants an' shirt on, but he couldn't get those wet boots over his wet socks. Ol' Tex, he tugged an' tugged an' nothin' happened. Finally ol' Tex turned to the nightstand by the bed an' got some of that vaseline—you know, what the gals keep there by the bed—an' he just greased up both his bare feet. An' goldurned if those boots didn't jist slide on as easy as if they was dry.

They Walked Away
from the Ambulance

COWBOYIN' WASN'T EASY, an' neither was ridin' the rodeos. Anyone who did either, or both, got his share of bangs. Why, I guess I was always skinned up. A guy was always skinned up, but unless you was hurt bad, hurt truly an' really bad, why you didn't pay no attention to them hurts.

There was one time I thought I'd really had it. Had a horse fall with me at the rodeo in Prescott one time. Turned over backwards on me. Like the old sayin' was, they had to pack me off to keep me from stinkin'. I was that dead, you know. Up there at Prescott, like they do at other rodeo places, they had a kind'a hospital deal. They didn't have an ambulance there those days, so they took me over to the little hospital in the buildin' there.

An' ol' Jack Burden, the guy I was dudin' for down there at Wickenburg, come a-runnin' over an' I could hear him talkin'. I'd been out, but I come to an' I could hear 'em talkin'. An' ol' Jack was sayin', "Do anythin' you have to." An' I could hear 'em talkin' about me, an' they said, "Well, we may have to operate on him. His stomach is all smashed in."

Now, these days they don't have saddle horns on those association saddles; they've made 'em without saddle horns since the fifties, so if the horse falls on the rider he won't get that goldurn horn in his guts. But back then there was a horn, an' what happened was that the swell of that saddle must have drove right up into my guts when that durn horse fell on me.

Well, there I was layin' there on that table, or that bed—I never knew which—an' I heard that feller say, "Well, we may have to operate on him."

That was all I had to hear. "Heck, there ain't anybody goin' to operate on me," I says. I got up an' walked out of there, by golly.

There was a lot of other times I got busted up, but I jist wouldn't go to those doctors or hospitals. You can see this one arm's kind'a curved an' I can show you a few other lumps from broken bones, but no hurt ever killed me when I was cowboyin' or rodeoin'.

Well, after I walked out of that durned hospital that day, I walked over an' got in the grandstand. Sore? I was jist sore as a boil. Dave Hill, my ol' buddy, an' I had kind'a teamed up there at Prescott. You know, we split any money we won. Well, I couldn't ride any more there at Prescott, an' he'd got bucked off his first horse. So Dave, he goes on up to Winslow to the rodeo there. I didn't go 'cause I was pretty badly banged up.

But the funny part is that they sent back word from Winslow —I got word that his horse had fell on him an' killed him. An' his mother an' his four sisters, they'd heard it, too. They was all disturbed about it.

What did happen was that his horse fell on him an' he was plumb knocked out. An' they put ol' Dave Hill in somethin' like an ambulance an' they was gonna cart him out to the hospital there in Winslow. Well, that goldurn Dave Hill, he just jumped out of that ambulance an' they didn't even know he was gone!

LX

I always loved rodeoin'. You see it's somethin'—well, it's a challenge. I guess if you want to be really an' truly honest about it, a man, actually everybody, has a certain amount of violence in him. An' a certain amount of ego, too, I guess. Well, you say what does a man want to fight for? Heck, I can remember that actually you jist wanted to fight. You jist picked a fight with somebody you knew jist 'cause you wanted to fight.

Well, it's kind'a the same way in the rodeo business. You had some of that violence in you, an' you jist wanted to go out there an' take it out on that goldurn buckin' horse, or that wild ol' steer.

It's a lot different today. In the olden days all those rodeo hands was cowboys from ranches, but today a lot of these top hands are graduates of colleges an' rodeo schools. Things sure can change around in this here world. But I'll tell you, I've watched some of these young ones an' a lot of 'em would make jist as good workin' cowboys as the old hands. But they jist don't have the big outfits anymore that have lots of wild cattle an' bad horses. There ain't no place to learn except rodeo school an' some of those little cow outfits.

Cowboyin'
Ain't What It Used to Be

IN THE SPRING when I'd get through wranglin' dudes at Wickenburg at the Remuda Ranch, I usually went to Prescott an' picked up my partner, ol' Dave Hill, an' we'd get off to them White Hills by ourselves. Dave and his dad had cattle in that area. Dave's dad had the Seven Up Ranch an' Dave had his own brand, the Lovin' U's.

We used to camp out there in Bull's Canyon before anybody else got in there, an' we used to brand everythin' we saw down there. You see, it was the kind'a country where everybody was stealin' from everybody else and you couldn't do nothin' much about it. A lot of the guys would spend all their time tryin' to ketch one guy stealin' one of their big calves while another guy was stealin' two of his.

It was a kind'a mixed-up affair, an' what it came down to was first come, first served. You got in there an' jist caught what steers you could an' led 'em out and branded whatever calves you saw. An' if you got caught, well, it was jist a mistake.

Right in the middle of this place was an ol' cowboy from Globe, ol' John Loveless, an' he had a deformed hand but he must'a been quite a cowboy from all the cattle he stole. He had drove in about forty head of cows all the way from Globe, across the Santa Maria, clear over to the ol' Neal Ranch on Burro Creek an' right straight up Burro Creek. An' he moved into what they called the mouth of Orejana Canyon, an' that's where he settled down and staked a homestead claim. He was right in the middle of about four outfits an' he could steal from all of 'em.

Dave an' I was workin' down there this one spring, an' we thought we'd ride in there an' see ol' Loveless. Well, we rode over there, an' here was this log house, an' he had this gal who hadn't been out of there much an' she was a little on the wild side. So we rode up there an' asked where John was, an' she said, "Oh, John? Oh, he's out tryin' to ketch a beef. We run outta meat an' he's out tryin' to ketch a beef." An' then she says, "Won't you get off your horses an' wait? I got a pot of beans on the stove an' you can have some lunch."

Well, we got down, an' durn if she didn't have one of those ol' phonographs with the cylinders. She started playin' some crazy ol' tunes an' she was talkin' away a mile a minute an' we was eatin' them beans. Pretty soon here came ol' John Loveless. He was ridin' a mule, a white mule. We said howdy an' asked him if he'd caught a beef.

An' he said, "Nah, I couldn't ketch one on this mule."

Ol' Dave, after we'd finished eatin', said, "Hell, I'll ketch you a beef if you can't ketch one on that mule."

I didn't think much of it, but we took off up Orejana Canyon an', by golly, we jumped a bunch of cattle up there about a mile or two. So there's a big ol' fat Yolo heifer in the bunch that would make a good beef. Ol' Dave caught that heifer an' says, "John, here's your beef. Jist take her on home."

Of course that heifer didn't belong to us or to John, an' we all knew that. But John says, "Thanks, I'll take her on home." He jist put his rope on her an' led that heifer down the canyon out of there.

I was a little bothered of givin' that beef to John 'cause I knew who it belonged to. "Golly, Dave," I said, "I don't think you should have caught that heifer an' given it to him."

[94]

An' ol' Dave, why he jist grinned. "Don't worry yourself any," Dave says to me. "Why John ain't gonna butcher that heifer. When he came in there to camp he had already caught his beef. He'd probably run onto our tracks an' knew we was down there at his cabin. He jist wasn't goin' to bring that beef in there when we knew it didn't belong to him. Hell, you can bet he's got a beef tied up somewhere, an' I'll bet you he'll turn that heifer loose before he gets a half-mile out of our sight. Then he'll go over an' get that beef he had tied up."

An' that's jist what it was all about. Ol' Dave, he understood what was goin' on.

$$\overline{+}$$

There's a lot of funny things about cowboyin', an' I guess you was never really finished learnin'. Like this business of left-handed ropers—you see, I'm a left-handed roper. Well, ol' Elsa Brown was a left-handed roper, an' you know, all the ropes are twisted to the right.

I never thought much about that 'til one time I was helpin' gather some brahmas at Yava for Madeline Jacob's outfit, an' this fella, Chappo Wayne, had a coupla ropes that was handmade over in Italy an' he jist couldn't do nothin' with 'em. They'd jist kink up on him an' everythin'. An' one day I picked up one an' put a loop in it, an' boy, that thing worked jist swell. An' I looked at that rope from Italy an' it was twisted to the left.

One time later on I was talkin' to a rope salesman an' I said, "You know, there's a lot of left-handed ropers an' they're always havin' trouble with their ropes. An' the simple reason is they're all twisted to the right. That's why they get so many kinks. Why don't you get your company to twist up some left-handed ropes?" Well, I guess that salesman thought I was crazy. But the fact is that was a real problem for left-handed ropers, an' I know, 'cause I'm a left-handed roper.

[95]

Now, there was this business of workin' horses on the mesas south of the headquarters of the Horseshoe outfit. The Forest Service said there were too many horses there, so the Ryans had to get rid of quite a few of 'em. There were lots of old mares that had iron rings on the top of their hoofs below the ankles of their front feet, so they couldn't run too fast. The ring was made to clamp around the ankle, an' when they did run the ring would hit the top of the hoof an' slow 'em up. Blacksmiths made those durn things, or you could do it yourself usin' horseshoes.

Well, we worked them horses from a holdup jist as we did cattle an' kept them in a holdin' pasture each night, an' what we wanted to take to Phoenix we put in a big pasture at the ranch. Ol' Elsa Brown was the boss of the horse roundup. We would corral each bunch we gathered in a day, an' that's when Elsa would ketch what horses he thought was started or broke. Before the Ryans took over the ranch, there had been lots of horses started then turned out. Nobody knew too much about what was out there. He would ketch one, an' if the horse led out, I saddled him up an' rode him some. Sure got a lot of bronc-ridin' practice.

An' that ol' Elsa Brown, he'd get into that corral an' he'd say, "Well, that looks like a god-danged horse that's been rode." Yep, he'd rope that thing, an' then I'd put my saddle on him an' I rode those durned ol' horses to find out whether they was broke or not. An' sometimes they'd really give you a fit. Like this time Elsa—I guess he was about six-feet-two—got into that corral, an' he roped this big ol' horse an' his rope was tied hard an' fast. But that horse wasn't goin' to give no way. Wasn't anythin' gonna stop him. He jist lit out an' broke that rope at the hondo, an' the damnedest thing you ever saw happened.

Why that goldurn broken hondo flew back an' hit ol' Elsa right in the forehead, knocked him plumb off his horse. By golly, I thought that rope had killed him deader 'n heck. But he finally got up. He was a big guy, an' durned if he didn't go right after that ol' horse again.

An' this ol' Elsa Brown I was tellin' you about, he was a-runnin' the Club Ranch up in the Mazatzals, an' when he got one of those wild ol' cows, know what he did? Why, to keep track of 'em he'd put bells on 'em, an' when you was out in that country you could hear 'em even when they was out in the thickets, in the brush.

Sometimes it was tough gettin' 'em out of the thickets an' what we'd do, goldurn it, was jist to set those brushes a-fire to get those cows out of there.

An' we had an ol' boy by the name of Pete Nail who was one of the wildest guys I ever saw. I seen that guy bringin' stock down that brush—he'd jist get his feet up under him in the saddle an' come through that high brush that way. I never did figure how he stayed on that horse.

Talk about learnin' how to handle them cattle, I remember when we was workin' for the Horseshoe, an' they was tryin' to gather in all the cattle. They figured they'd build these traps; they called 'em salt traps. That's where you built a trap on salt grounds, make it out of these cypress poles, jist kinda like a fence, but you had poles across the top an' you had a gate. They was called triggers. You had these poles that fit together an' swung open when somethin' went through there. When a cow went through, why those triggers closed. After you got the cattle trapped, you still had trouble on your hands. Those cattle could be pretty wild, an' you'd have to rope an' lead 'em out to a holding pasture. An' when you got those cattle goin' on the drive, you had to know what you was doin'. If you ever tried to stop 'em real quick, why they'd scatter like a bunch of quail. So you kind'a had to go with 'em 'til they learned how to be driven.

I remember an ol' steer one time broke out right between Floyd Orr an' me. He was a wild hand, that boy, but I didn't pay no attention to him. I knew what you had to do. You didn't want to run anythin' very far. You had to ketch somethin' right goldang quick. Well, I caught this steer; I'm left-handed, so I caught him with my left hand. Floyd was right-handed, an' I guess he didn't pay any attention to me an' run right out there an' caught that steer right on the top of my rope.

Here both of us are out catchin' the same steer an' them cattle was jist goin' all around us. Really an' truly, that was a mess out there until those other guys—you had to have more cowboys in front than any place else—they all came around an' finally got the cattle held up.

Then there was the story of what happened to ol' Bill Coburn. Bill had the Horseshoe Ranch, and he was the half-brother of the western writer, Walt Coburn. There was a ranch up there under the rim called the MT, up above the Verde River, an' Walt stayed up there for a while. I think that's where he wrote his first western story, at this ol' MT Ranch. A couple or three months before he died I asked ol' Walt why he hadn't written a story about his brother an' his outfit.

An' Walt said, "Well, Frank, I never did know what the whole deal was. I went into the army in 1918 an' then to California after the war."

The fact is, that was quite a story. That ol' Bill Coburn, he had come to Arizona from Montana an' jist practically bought up every ranch in that whole area in the Bloody Basin. He really had put together a big outfit, but he'd had to borrow about a million dollars an' I guess he finally saw he couldn't make a go of it 'cause he owed so much money. I think this was durin' World War I, an' he couldn't hire a lot of cowboys, so he was importin' a lot of these Mexican cowboys up there.

There is this story among the ol'-timers . . . Bill had gathered up about 2,500 of the best cattle he had in the whole durned outfit an' got permission to ship 'em to feed. But he didn't say where he was a-goin' to ship 'em. Some people say he'd taken the lot an' some of the best horses, too, an' shipped 'em all to Mexico, an' went down there with 'em an' took out naturalization papers. Well, they couldn't do a thing to him, an' so the outfit that loaned him the money was jist stuck. But ol' Bill, why he was safe down there in Mexico.

I was down Phoenix way the other day, an' I was rememberin' when we used to trail cattle to Glendale. They don't do it anymore, but I can remember when we'd drive a bunch of cows an' calves an' steers an' bulls from the Verde River an' come across that Paradise Valley—why there wasn't anythin' out there then, an' now there's all them big, fancy homes. Well, we'd come right across that Paradise Valley when there wasn't a thing out in that country.

We would have probably seven or eight hundred head, an'

we'd come across the canal an' go down Fifty-first Avenue an' cross over Grand Avenue to get to the stockyards in Glendale. An', golly, we'd jist hold up all the traffic. Can you imagine what would happen today if you tried to drive a bunch of cattle down through Paradise Valley into Glendale an' across Grand Avenue? Why, you'd have the biggest mess on your hands you ever saw.

No, sir, cowboyin' ain't what it used to be, an' it ain't ever again gonna be the way it was. Jist no more.

I've Seen Horses Smarter 'n Men

PEOPLE ARE ALWAYS askin' me if I think animals are smart. Like they ask, "Can a horse or a mule think?" Well, cows, horses, an' mules, really an' truly, I don't think they can think. Now, I've seen some awfully smart animals, but whether they think things out, I can't say. I don't know. I've seen some horses that was awful smart, but they all go by instinct. Actually, they're controlled by a higher power, an' that's why you have to believe in a power greater than your own self. You take a person, a baby, you got to take care of that baby. It don't know a thing. It's got a lot to learn from the humans, you understand what I mean. Sure, it has certain instincts about suckin' its mother, you know, an' some other things which are instincts. But as a matter of fact, human people are born with very, very few instincts, in my opinion, while animals are all born with a lot of instincts. That's what they run by.

Now mules are smarter than horses. Burros are smarter than horses. They're born with what you call a self-preservation instinct. They're born to really look after themselves. They're stubborn. An' a burro ain't a-gonna run himself to death like a horse will.

Now there's certain ways of breakin' a horse. In the ol' days a horse breaker had a certain way of breakin' horses, which was just knockin' the buck out of 'em. Back years ago they didn't have corrals. They just tied 'em up, or staked 'em, an' that's why they had so many bad horses, you see. They tried to teach 'em all the same.

Horses has got instincts, but still an' all they are jist kind'a like people; they all have their own individuality. They're all different from one another, you see.

People are the same way. Like if you're workin' a crew, you can't treat every one of 'em the same. There are all different kinds of people. Why, you have to be half-psychiatrist to figure out how to handle this guy, how to handle that guy. The same with horses. Horse breakin's got to be a kind'a science. There's certain rules an' regulations that you go by, but you have to handle one horse one way an' another horse a different way. You got to learn what you can do with this horse an' what you can do with another horse. Why years ago, they jist didn't do that; they was handlin' horses all the same.

I'll tell you about one of the smarter horses I ever saw, an' that was a big ol' horse called Pumpkin that my friend, Dave Hill, had.

This ol' Pumpkin was the best lead horse I ever saw in my life. He was a smart son of a gun. When you're leadin' out wild cattle, you tie up a steer to a horse an' lead him out of the rough country. An', say, when you're goin' up a hill, that goddamn steer might stop. When that happens, why you got off your horse an' jog that goldurn steer with a stick right behind the front shoulder. What made Pumpkin so special was that he knew just how to handle the rope. Whenever that steer would move, Pumpkin would move right with him an' never tighten the rope.

The main thing in leadin' is you can't get nobody close behind you 'cause the steer wants to turn around an' fight 'em. Now, when you're leadin' you never drag a steer or tighten your rope; the only time to do that is when he's goin' away from you, an' then you jist jerk him back. An' that ol' Pumpkin, he understood every move you made. He was a natural-born lead horse. That was one smart ol' horse.

Talkin' about smart horses, take trainin' animals. A lot of times you leave a horse alone an' he'll learn more by himself than in tryin' to teach him. People are the same way sometimes.

That takes me back to when I was a kid an' a-trainin' all kinds of animals. You'd be surprised how easy most of 'em takes to trainin'. When I was just a young kid I had a burro that I taught to do all kinds of tricks: untie knots, lay down an' roll over, tell how old she was, an' jist—jist shut up, too. I've always been a pretty good hand with trainin'. There was the time they was puttin' on an Elk's circus down there in Phoenix, an' so I trained two Roman ridin' mules for the show an' also an ol' pig that would pull a wagon around. I got the pig from the ol' Central Avenue dairy.

Why, I had that pig trained so well that the durn thing would foller me all over. I had him an' a jumpin' mule trained for the circus, an' I had a kind of a clown suit. But that pig, he jist wouldn't let me get out of his sight. That son of a gun knew his name, Ted, an' he'd foller me up to the pool hall at Five Points. Act jist like a dog. Well, I'd send him on home an' doggone if he wouldn't jist peek around the corner of the buildin's to watch where I was goin'. I tried to leave him at the dairy after the circus folded, but it wasn't easy. That pig, that goldurn pig, jist didn't want to leave me.

But the fact is, I was more interested in horses anyway, an' one time I was out there at Agua Caliente, Hot Springs. They had a lot of wild horses, mustangs, really. Golly, I was jist a kid, but I was crazy about horses, you know, like a kid will be. An' they had a little black horse they'd caught, a mustang. "Golly," I said, "I'd sure like to ride that one."

Well, the fellers out there, they knew that was a wild one, so they said, "I'll tell you what we'll do. We'll saddle him up, an' if you can ride him you can have him."

So I says, "All right. Fine."

I didn't even have a pair of boots at that time. I was jist wearin' an ol' pair of shoes. So they saddled him up, an' actually they were bein' wise guys puttin' a kid on a horse they knew would buck. But they didn't want me to get hurt, so in place of lettin' him loose they jist let him out on a long rope. By golly, the durn son of a gun bucked me off an' I hung a foot, you know, with that ol' shoe I was wearin', hung a foot in the stirrup.

So they pulled up on that horse an' got me out of that, but I said, "Let me back on that son of a gun." An' so I got back on him, an', by golly, I rode him that time. An' doggone if they didn't give me that little black horse.

MT

Now, I've seen some horses that was smarter then men. For instance, horses will jist come home by themselves. I've seen that. In fact, there's horses know how to get back home better than cowboys. They jist have an instinct. Like at night on the trail, lots of times you jist give your horse his head an' he'll take you in. Whether they can see after dark, I can't say. I jist say it's instinct, a natural instinct they're born with.

An' cows, well, cows ain't dumb. They're pretty smart. Their feed an' water an' salt are the main things for cattle. You git water an' salt for 'em an' they will always find feed if there is any. I remember when they used to have lots of cattle on Bozarth Mesa where the grass was a foot an' a half high, an' the cattle that stayed there had to walk clear to the bottom of the canyon to get water. By the time they got back up there on the mesa they was dry again, an' they wouldn't eat. So that's why ranchers got to buildin' tanks down there, dams in some draws to ketch the water.

Now the dumbest animals in the world are gentle cattle. If you really want to see a dumb cow, why jist look at a goldurn gentle cow that was raised by people an' not put out there to care for theirselves, to rustle for theirselves. I remember the time I was workin' for these guys, an' they took to feedin' these ol' cows this one winter an' then they turned them out. But those cows, they jist wouldn't rustle anymore; they jist stayed around where they was took care of. Like a lot of these milk cows, you turn 'em out to rustle for theirselves an' they'll jist starve to death. But those ol'-time cattle would sure rustle.

An' that's why there's so many cattle that are crossbred today. Brahmas will rustle, an' now they got what they call Brangus cattle—they're part Brahma an' part what they call this Angus. An' believe me, they're a good rustlin' cattle. You won't find 'em starvin' theirselves to death if there is any feed at all.

∩

Let me tell you about how smart some of these wild cattle can be. Like the time we was workin' down on the Verde River, an' these cattle had run into thick mesquite an' was jist havin' one helluva good time eatin' those mesquite beans. Well, we wanted to get those cattle out, but you can't take a horse into those goldurn mesquite thickets—jist tear you an' your horse plumb apart. So what you did was to put a couple of guys alongside the outside of the thicket, an' then you'd get off your horse an' let somebody lead him, an' then come down through this thicket a-foot. Then the rest of the guys is all waitin' with their loops built in their ropes 'cause you've got to ketch these cattle before they get out of one thicket an' right back into another.

Now, I don't know whether you want to call these cattle jist smart, or whether they was actin' out of instinct. But I'll tell you, here you were a-comin' through that goldurn mesquite thicket an' you could hear those cattle a-knockin' down limbs of trees. You'd get down to the middle where you heard them, an' all of a sudden you wouldn't hear a sound. You wouldn't hear a goldurn thing. So you'd start up again, an' you'd hear them cattle plowin' through the brush, but when you'd stop, it all got quiet again.

What was happenin' was them goldurn things would sneak around you, lay down an' jist be as quiet as heck until you went right by 'em, you see. An' then those goldurn things would jist go on back behind you. Now whether that is instinct, or they figured it out for theirselves I couldn't say. An' I have seen an awful lot of times where those goldurn cattle seem to try to out-figure you. An' you'd call them dirty, mean cattle every name in the book.

Really an' truly, a cowboy had to learn to read a cow's mind, to know what that damn thing was thinkin'. An' the same way for a good horse breaker; he's got to know for sure what that horse is thinkin'. An' with a mule, the thinkin' is different; that's why a lot of good horse breakers can't get along with a mule at all. You got to understand each one of those goldurn animals. You kind'a have to be half jackass yourself to get along with them.

-U-

As I say, it's kind'a bad comparin' animals with people, but really an' truly, they're the same. A person is just an advanced form of an animal—you know what I mean. The only thing is that a person, well, he's jist born with a lot more sense. But he has to learn the same way as animals.

{ 107 }

Now you take a newborn calf, a-layin' around with a bunch of cows. Of a sudden those cows are a-wantin' some water, so they'll parade down to where the water is. The calves don't need water, those little ones, so they stay right there. An', by golly, if them cows don't leave one or two cows as baby-sitters. One or two cows will stay with them calves while the rest of 'em will go to water. An' those calves will stay right there.

I can't really explain it. I don't think them calves have much in the way of brains, but they'll stay right there. Heck, many a time I've seen two cows an' about ten calves with 'em.

An' I'll tell you somethin' else. If a calf gets separated from the cow, or the other way around, why you can be sure they'll both go back to the same place where they was last together.

R

There is horses an' mules that will take a likin' to a particular person. Heck, I had this trained burro when I was a kid. Why she'd jist follow me all over. An' there were plenty of times when I'd go out to the corral where she was an' she jist started to brayin'. She was jist that glad to see me. Yes, sir, they do develop a lot of affection for people. They sure do. An' then I've seen horses an' mules an' such that wouldn't have nothin' to do with certain people, nothin' to do with 'em at all. Like they have an ol' sayin', "If you see a guy, an' dogs an' animals or children don't like him, stay clear of him, 'cause there's somethin' the matter with that guy."

Golly, I've had horses an' mules that would jist foller me around in the corral. Heck, take this ol' saddle mule that I won all the ribbons with. I kept that ol' mule in a pasture, an' when I'd be out irrigatin' in that pasture that mule would jist foller me all over the place. An' if I didn't pay no attention to him, why he'd nudge me in the back.

Frank Polk
an' the Singin' Pig

I GOT TO SINGIN' when I was down there around Wickenburg workin' for Jack Burden's ol' Remuda Ranch. Well, we used to go on those moonlight rides, take those dudes out in the desert, you know, for a ride an' steak fry. Well, we'd get out there around a fire, an' I took to singin'. I'd learned a few songs, a few cowboy songs, an' so I got to singin'.

Ol' Jack Burden's mother-in-law, she heard me one time, an' she says to me, "Golly, Frank, you got a pretty good voice." She played a guitar, an' she said, "I'll get you a guitar an' I'll teach you how to chord."

An' that's where I really got to playin' the guitar an' singin'. An' I wouldn't learn the regular songs, you know; I'd learn songs from the ol' cowboys. Heck, I'd follow a guy around a week or two 'til I learned the goldurn thing.

By golly, I even was on the radio a-singin'. But there was this little incident that happened in 1938 or '37, I forget which. Down in Phoenix on KOY, ol' Jack Williams was the announcer. That ol' boy became governor later on. Well, we had a regular program called *The Ranch Hour,* an' it came on at seven o'clock in the morning. We had a pretty good deal, even if they wasn't payin' much.

Well, about that time I had a little pig, a goldurn singin' pig. I had quite a feelin' for pigs. I'd trained quite a few, like that one that used to foller me around when I was a kid. Well, I trained this little pig an' you could take him an' you could play him like an accordion. You'd squeeze him an' he'd squeal hard. An' then when you let up, why, he'd kind'a give out a wheeze. Of course, when I'd squeeze him hard he could let out a hell of a loud squeal, an' those technicians in behind the studio window, why, they'd be wavin' at me to get that goldurn pig away from the microphone or else he'd blow a fuse or somethin'.

An' I'd also take that pig down to the Fox Theatre in Phoenix —it's all tore down now—where we had a weekly stage show. Well, I'd put that pig inside my guitar case an' they'd announce me as Frank Polk, the singer.

An' what I'd do is get out in front of this microphone, put the guitar case down, an' then pull the durn pig out of the case. An' the crowd would jist go wild.

About this time I wasn't doin' much drinkin', oh, a beer or two, but nothin' much more. Heck, I'd been singin' for about two months on KOY an' I'd stayed sober. People never even knew I was a drinker. So there was a fellow by the name of Jackie Kennedy, an' he ran one of those chuck wagon diners—had a wagon fixed up in a truck, an' he'd put on these chuck wagon dinners for the dudes. He charged a high price for that dinner—I guess it was a dollar an' a half. But, no kiddin', that was a high price in those days. Well, he'd hired me to go out there an' sing those cowboy songs to the dudes an', well, one night I got drunk. Man, I really got drunk out there. About ten o'clock that night we came in from there, came into town; still had this pig with me, an' we made for the bars. We was up there at the Westward Ho, where they had a kind'a circular bar. Well, it wasn't long before I had that durn pig a-runnin' around that bar. That was some sight to see, that little ol' pig runnin' around that circular bar at that fancy hotel!

After they closed the bar we went over to this Kennedy feller's house an' started in on a bottle. We got just drunker than skunks. Well, I had to go down to Jack Williams's radio show over KOY at seven in the mornin' an' it was already early in the mornin'. So I said to Jackie, "Come on down to the radio station. I'll get a world of publicity for your chuck wagon dinners."

We got down there to that station, opened the door to the studio an' there was ol' Jack Williams. He'd just been sayin', "I wonder where Frank's at? He's late gettin 'here." Then he looks up at me comin' in with that pig under my arm.

That was the time they used to put the microphone right in the middle of the goldurn studio an' they had those big plush rugs on the floor. So I came in there with that pig under my arm an' ol' Jack Williams, he didn't know I was drunk. I set that little pig down on this goldurn rug, an' that durn son of a gun, I don't know why he picked on that microphone, but he just walked

around that microphone an' jist pissed a circle around that microphone.

If Jack Williams had kept his mouth shut, I probably wouldn't have popped off like I did. But right there, right over that microphone takin' that program all over the durn state, he says, "Oh, Frank, your pig isn't housebroken."

An' I jist pops right back with, "Well, the son of a gun hasn't pissed all night."

That went all over the goldurn country, an' that was the end, jist the end, of my singin' career on radio. But hell, I wasn't makin' very much money anyway.

Jist Artistically Inclined

I GUESS I WAS ALWAYS artistically inclined. Heck, when I was a kid I used to draw pictures—in school, an' everywhere else, too. All the art teachers at school used to send home notes to my mother sayin', "You ought'a send this boy to art school." But then after I got outta there, well, that drawin' kind'a ended when I got out of school. I guess I got too much interested in cowboyin' an' rodeoin' an' forgot all about drawin' pictures.

But then when I went to work at Rainbow Natural Bridge—I guess that was back in the late twenties—why I was packin' people in to see that place. I stayed up there all winter, an' there was a lot of time for jist settin' around. Well, I jist got to drawin' pictures of the Navajos, the visitors, an' the cowboys that came around the place.

An' then when I went to Hollywood an' got sick, as I told you, I couldn't do anythin' heavy in work, so I got started with wood carvin'. That was when my wife bought that apartment house out there an' I had kind of a shop down in the basement where I'd fix furniture. But this friend of mine who was an illustrator for a magazine, why, he said to me one day, "If you're gonna get well, Frank, you're gonna have to set out here in the sun." An' this feller, why, his hobby was wood carvin', an' all he ever carved was madonnas. An' he says to me, "Frank, you're kind'a artistic. Why don't you get some kind'a hobby?"

Well, pretty soon he had me whittlin', an' we'd be a-settin' out there on the steps of that apartment—him carvin' away on his madonnas an' me, I'd whittle out these cowboys an' these horses. They wasn't very good; really an' truly, they was very crude. But that's where I got started in art. I really got into wood carvin' after that an' I stayed in it all except durin' World War II. I couldn't go in the army 'cause I was 4-F, but I worked in defense.

After the war was over, then I went back up to Reno an' I got strictly into wood carvin'. An' then after I got into the Cowboy Artists of America, which was about in '67, I jist quit the wood carvin' entirely an' went to workin' in wax for my bronze figures.

You know, I was a lucky son of a gun. Never had an art lesson in school in my life. Never went to art school. But I worked with a lot of good artists an' they really helped me, like that ol' Tex Wheeler who did that life-size figure of ol' Seabiscuit—or Citation, I forget which—over at that Santa Anita race track in California. He was a great friend of mine an' he helped me a lot. So did ol' J. R. Williams, that great western cartoonist.

I was really a lucky son of a gun.

OO

The first thing I ever sold was up there in Reno. I had made some wood carvin's an' they was settin' up behind a bar, you know, in the saloon. I was askin' fifteen dollars for each figure, an' this guy looks at them an' says to me, "Why, I wouldn't give you ten dollars."

An' I shot back at him, "Hell, I wouldn't even take ten dollars."

But the very next day, a friend of mine, Charlie Lattimore, who was handlin' dudes out at the next ranch, called an' says to me, "Frank, what do you want for them two wood carvin's?"

I guess I kind'a had my hackles up by then, an' I said, "I want twenty-five dollars apiece for 'em."

An', by golly, if this woman out there at the dude ranch didn't buy both of 'em. That was the first time I sold anythin' I made, an' I guess I'll always remember that little incident. Kind'a get to thinkin' about that now when I sell off one of my bronzes for four figures, you know.

EVERY WAY BUT LOOSE 1974 Bronze

It's funny how you can remember those little things when you start lookin' back.

Like, I remember goin' to that big high school down there in Phoenix. Barry Goldwater was goin' to that school, an' actually I was in his class, his English class. Why I remember that they had a guy who was a pretty good artist, Reg Manning, an' he used to come over to that school, give talks an' do a little drawin'. An' I guess when you look back on it, that, too, got somethin' a-workin' in the back of my brain.

A LONG ROPE AND A TELESCOPE 1975 Bronze

[116]

Actually, when it comes to my art I'm a great hand for authenticity. There's been so much phony stuff on the market that it makes you kind'a sick to the stomach at times. This western art has got pretty popular lately, an' I guess that's why you see so much of this phony stuff. It looks like everybody has got to doin' this old-time cowboy stuff, you know, jist goin' back to Charlie Russell an' Remington an' a few other guys from that time.

When I got started, really an' truly, there wasn't too many doin' cowboy art in particular. Oh, there was Tex Wheeler, but he'd never cowboyed in this particular area. He was raised in Florida an' he'd come in here from Texas. An' there was another artist, ol' Jack Van Ryder. He was as good an ol' painter as I ever

RIM-FIRED IN BLOODY BASIN   1976   Bronze

saw. For a long time, why, he was just a-trampin' around until this hat company picked him up, by golly, backed him, an' got him to illustratin' all their catalogues. But ol' Jack, he was truly a cowboy an' a rodeo hand. There was a few other western artists around in that day, but really an' truly, there wasn't a lot of what I'd call cowboy artists at that time.

When I first started in carvin' I did a lot of rodeo stuff, 'cause I rodeoed quite a lot. I was workin' from actual experience. An' when I was up there on the Indian reservation I did a lot of pictures of Indians, Navvies. You know, Navajo Indians. An' at that time I jist drawed things I saw, but I never thought of doin' anythin' as far as the cowboy angle. To me, that was just a matter of doin' a day's work. It didn't seem that important to me from an art standpoint.

But, by golly, when I think of it, if a guy'd just had a camera with him in those days—of course, you wouldn't had time, goldurn it, to take pictures when you was workin'—jist imagine the pictures you could have taken of what was happenin'. Like leadin' them cattle, tyin' them cattle down, an' movin' wild cattle. An' horses—taken pictures of them wild, buckin' horses. If somebody'd had jist enough sense to go to one of those outfits with a movie camera an' taken in everythin', why, they'd have a picture that'd be worth a million dollars right now.

Actually the only time they'd taken pictures in those days was when a guy was a-settin' still on a horse. Nobody ever thought of doin' it differently, an' I guess if they was to have tried here in Arizona, with all them hills, mountains, an' deep canyons, why they'd have to shoot durned quick anyway.

When I got started in western art there wasn't a lot of guys doin' more than copyin', 'cause they didn't have the experiences theirselves. So I got to thinkin' about this, an' I said to myself, "All they're doin' is goin' back an' copyin' Russell's stuff an' Remin'ton's stuff." Actually, they had no ideas of their own. For instance, George Phippen was as fine a western artist as I ever saw, an' one time I asked him, "George, why don't you do some pictures of guys a-workin' these wild cattle, catchin' cattle when they stuck their heads out of the holdup, an' tippin' their horns an' stuff like that?"

An' he says, "Frank, I can't do it 'cause I never saw it. I never experienced it." An' he said he'd give anythin' in the world if he'd a had the chance to work at cowboyin' at the time that I was a-workin' the ranges. This guy really had cowboy in his heart, you know, but he never had the real experiences.

So I began thinkin' 'about what ol' George said. An', by golly, it was logical as heck. If you're doin' western art it can't come secondhand. To really be authentic, it can't come secondhand. So I jist said to myself, "Well, hell, from now on anythin' I do is goin' to be somethin' I did an' saw, somethin' I know that nobody in the world can tear apart." An' the fact is, if I kept workin' the rest of my life I couldn't get down the ideas from all that I saw or did when I was out there cowboyin'.

F C

Before I moved out of Nevada in '59 I'd been doin' jist carvin', as I said. I'd do anythin', I wasn't particular. I'd do cowboys, Indians, even carved a back bar of a dragon. They wanted this for a big ol' bar, an' they even went over to Hawaii to get a picture of the dragon they wanted me to copy. Not a real dragon, of course, but a carvin' of an ol' dragon over there. An' I was carvin' those ol' slot machine figures at that time, too. Then this feller Dick Graves, who owned the Golden Nugget up there in Nevada, wanted me to carve him a rooster. He was lookin' for some publicity an' they had what they called the Golden Rooster Room where they served strictly chicken. So they got the idea, why don't we have a golden rooster cast, see?

I wasn't particularly fond of the idea of makin' that rooster. I wasn't too fond of that, an' when they asked me how much I'd charge, why I said, "Heck, I won't charge you much; you're a friend of mine." I should have charged him a heckuva lot, but I only asked him for fifty dollars. For back then that was a pretty good bit of money, I guess. Well, I worked on it for about three or four days. I got some pictures of a rooster—you see, chickens is a bit out of my line; all I ever did with chickens was eat 'em. But I made that goldurn model an', by golly, if they didn't cast it by the lost wax process—in gold.

That damn thing was valued at $40,000. When they opened up that fancy restaurant room, why they had that golden chicken in a bullet-proof glass case. They got a lot of publicity out of it. They wrote a lot of things about it, an' some of the articles called it "Frank Polk's Chicken."

When I came down to Tucson I jist forgot all about that golden chicken. Then one day a guy comes to my door an' says he's from the Secret Service, an' he says, "I want to talk to you about that golden rooster."

You can bet I kind'a shook a bit. I said to myself, "Now what in the heck are they after me for?" Well, that agent explained that the government and the Secret Service was interested 'cause that durn old golden rooster came under the gold standard. See, you were just allowed to have so much gold at that time, an' the fact was that there was more gold on that goldurn rooster than anybody, outside of a jeweler, was supposed to have, unless it was a work of art. Just like them King Tut gold things—you can have 'em, but you got to prove they're art.

So what the government was tryin' to prove was that ol' Dick Graves had just picked up some model of a rooster an' had it cast in gold. That's what they thought. Well, I happened to have all the drawin's an' I started to talk to that agent. He told me that they had taken away that goldurn rooster, confiscated it, I think he said, an' had stuck it in the vault of a bank up there in Reno. They really got the publicity this time. You know, here was the golden rooster doin' time in jail, an' meanwhile they'd picked up another model an' just painted him gold an' put him in the real rooster's place.

Well, it jist turned out that this Secret Service agent was a wood carver by hobby, an' me an' him got along jist fine. I showed him all the drawin's an' write-ups, an' the next day when he came back, why he brought along some of his own wood carvin's to show me.

The way it turned out was the government had been tryin' to prove that the rooster wasn't a work of art, that they'd never heard of Frank Polk, that he wasn't an artist. But, by golly, they had to back down an' the case was won 'cause it was decided that the *Golden Rooster* was a work of art done by the artist Frank Polk.

+S

At this time, you see, most of what I was doin' was commercial art an' really an' truly, you had to do an awful lot of that to make a livin', 'cause western art jist wasn't sellin' that goldurn well. Anyhow, I went down there to Scottsdale to that O'Brien's Art Emporium—an' there was only about three galleries down there then an' now I think there's, oh, hell, about seventy of 'em. Well, I sold ol' Bill some of my wood carvin's. It was Bill said to me later on that he wasn't really crazy about the wood carvin's, but sure would like to have some cast in bronze. An' that's what started me off in doin' what I'm doin' today.

An' when I look back at the way things went, you know, all those wild days an' nights cowboyin' an' rodeoin', an' that damn alcoholism, I guess things kind'a turned out pretty good.

When I think about it—well, it's just like me to think of a little story. This one's about an' ol' cowboy who was a-runnin' horses an' damn if his ol' horse didn't fall with him into a gol-durned gully. This cowboy was a long ways from camp, an' it was gettin' dark. He'd broke his leg, an' this durn ol' horse was a-layin' there on top of him. Couldn't get up. He's wedged in there.

Well, this ol' cowboy had never prayed much—jist an ol' cow-boy, you know, who got drunk an' raised hell an' never thought much about religion or any goldurned thing like that. But now he got to thinkin', "Man, if I'm ever goin' to pray, then I guess this is the time. An' goldurn it, maybe I'd better pray right now."

So that ol' cowboy, he looks up an' he starts, "Goldurn, ol' Lord, I never asked you for nothin' in my life. But, by golly, I'm in pretty doggone bad shape, an' I need some help. Oh, Lord, I ain't never prayed before, but I sure wish you would come an' get me out of this goddamned storm."

Then as an afterthought he said, "Say, listen, you come yourself. Don't send your son Jesus, 'cause this ain't no job for a kid."

Now, that's a joke, but, you know, I've often thought about that, I tell you. You see, that's really the main thing about the AA —the Alcoholics Anonymous—you see, there's a higher power. What it is you can't explain, but it's all around you. It's a higher power, an' that's what I believe in, an' I'm a firm believer that that's what made it all work out for me in the end.

A Personal Note
from Frank Polk

WHEN THEY CAME AROUND to namin' this goldurn book, I had two suggestions. Durn if they didn't take neither one, so I'd like to tell you about them. My first idea was to call it "Frank Polk Tells It the Way It Was." You see, that's the way I've always been, tellin' it jist like it was an' I guess that's why people kind'a liked my storytellin'. An' then, by golly, I thought I ought to have somethin' for a title that really told it the way it was. So I suggested "Deep Tracks an' Thin Shit." Really an' truly, friends, when you was out there working wild cattle that's all you ever saw, an' them ol' cowboys had that for kind'a of a sayin'—deep tracks an' thin shit.

An' so if they ain't gonna use any of my titles, at least I'd like to dedicate this durned book to all the good cowboys I worked with, all the dudes I wrangled, all the people I caused so much trouble, all the people from AA that helped me so much.

But above all I want to dedicate this book to my wife, Mary, who gave me a new lease on life after our marriage in 1970; to my sister, Martha Irvine, who got all them pictures of the olden days for me; to Mary's sister, Mattie Cooper Nelson; and to Jack Morgan and Learah Cooper Morgan, who all did so goldurn much to help me get started again with my art after my long bout with sickness in California in 1972.

Frank entertaining fellow Cowboy Artists Bill Owen
(left) and Joe Beeler (center) with one of his many tales

DESIGNED BY MARK SANDERS
COMPOSED IN LINOTYPE GRANJON
WITH DISPLAY LINES
IN CALEDONIA
PRINTED ON WARREN'S OLDE STYLE
AT THE PRESS IN THE PINES

NORTHLAND PRESS

BOUND BY ROSWELL BOOKBINDING
PHOENIX